Dyslexia tools for Kids

Your help handbook for children, parents and teachers with fun exercises and tools for learning and improving the skills of dyslexic children

Angie Turner

© Copyright 2020 by Angie Turner. All right reserved.

The work contained herein has been produced with the intent to provide relevant knowledge and information on the topic on the topic described in the title for entertainment purposes only. While the author has gone to every extent to furnish up to date and true information, no claims can be made as to its accuracy or validity as the author has made no claims to be an expert on this topic. Notwithstanding, the reader is asked to do their own research and consult any subject matter experts they deem necessary to ensure the quality and accuracy of the material presented herein.

This statement is legally binding as deemed by the Committee of Publishers Association and the American Bar Association for the territory of the United States. Other jurisdictions may apply their own legal statutes. Any reproduction, transmission or copying of this material contained in this work without the express written consent of the copyright holder shall be deemed as a copyright violation as per the current legislation in force on the date of publishing and subsequent time thereafter. All additional works derived from this material may be claimed by the holder of this copyright.

The data, depictions, events, descriptions and all other information forthwith are considered to be true, fair and accurate unless the work is expressly described as a work of fiction. Regardless of the nature of this work, the Publisher is exempt from any responsibility of actions taken by the reader in conjunction with this work. The Publisher acknowledges that the reader acts of their own accord and releases the author and Publisher of any responsibility for the observance of tips, advice, counsel, strategies and techniques that may be offered in this volume.

Table of Contents

Introduction 7
#1 What It Means to Be Dyslexic   10
How reading happens 11
How a child learns to read 12
Symptoms 15
Adults and teens 18
When to go to your doctor 19
Diagnosing 19
Causes 21
Risk factors 22
Complications 23
Managing dyslexia 24
Making it easier for them 24
How children feel 25

#2 Give Them a Reason to Read   27
Setting up a token economy 28
What should tokens be? 31
Starting your token economy 31
Token economy chart 33
Response cost 34
Conditioned reinforcement 35
Risks 36

#3 Emotional Support   38
Overcoming Emotional Issues 41

#4 Set Routines   44
Dulling creativity and spontaneity 47
Should infants have routines 47

Benefits of routines 48
What is a good routine? 53
Ideas for toddler and preschool routines 53
Ideas for school-age children routines 54

#5 Read With Them 57
Bookshare... 61
Local libraries and schools............................. 62
Online help... 62
Difference between audiobooks and text-to-speech 63

#6 Get Multisensory 66
It isn't only a song and dance 69
Kinesthetic 69
Tactile 70
Auditory 70
Visual... 71
How to create a multisensory house.............. 72
Things you can do 75

#7 Create Homework Time 78
Homework strategies 80
How to create a homework station 85
What is a homework station? 86
Find the space 86
What your child needs 87
Get rid of clutter 88
Create a routine..90
Creating good habits 91
Homework supplies 92
Strategies to help homework go smoother 92
Incentive and reward program 93
Creating the incentive program 95

#8 Color Code 97
Colored overlays 99
Color coded schedules 101

#9 Reading Assisters 106
Reading strips 107
Line tracker 108
Visual tracker 109
Sight words 111
Online help for dyslexia 116

#10 Celebrate 120
Other types of success 121
Benefits of celebration 123
How to celebrate 123
How not to celebrate 126
Famous people with dyslexia 129

Conclusion 133

Introduction

First off, I would like to thank you for choosing this book, and I hope that both you and your child find it informative and helpful. The goal of this book is to present parents with information and tools for dyslexia that can help them and their child learn how to view this as not a problem, but a new way of viewing things. Why? Because I'm a mother of a dyslexic girl and I became a tutor for children with learning disabilities and I want help you with some important advice.

We will start things out by discussing what it means to be dyslexic. We will look at demystifying some of the beliefs about dyslexia so that you have a clear understanding of what it is and isn't. Then the rest of the book will be focused on different strategies that help the dyslexic child.

First, we will look at ways to help get your child reading. Most children with dyslexic are reluctant to read because they find it difficult, so giving them some incentive to read can help.

Then we will move into discussing the importance of a routine. Routines are great for any child, but for a child with dyslexia, they can be what helps them to overcome the struggle. After that, we will talk about reading with them. The goal is to get your child comfortable with reading, right? One way to do so is to use audiobooks and to read with them.

Next, we'll look at how to use multisensory lessons to help your child. Getting more than one sense involved can help them learn better. Then we will discuss how to create homework time. Homework tends to be a big struggle for parents and children because the child is exhausted from the brainpower they had to use at school, so this chapter will help you to work through that problem together.

The next thing we will look at is emotional support for your child. This is something that gets overlooked because it isn't always obvious, but most children with dyslexia will need some sort of emotional support. There are many different reasons for this, and we will look at each of them and what to do.

Then we'll talk about color coding things. Color code appears in many different ways for a dyslexic child, such as color coding schedules, to colored overlays to help them read. Either way, color helps with dyslexia.

After that, we will look at reading assisters for a dyslexic child. These will be various tools that they can use that will help them when reading, such as reading strips.

Lastly, we'll go over the importance of celebrating your child's successes. Dyslexic children tend to lack confidence in themselves, but you can help them overcome this through celebrating. Every child likes to know that their parent is happy with what they are doing, and this tends to be even more important for a child with dyslexia. With that, let's begin.

#1

What It Means to Be Dyslexic

To put it simply, dyslexia is a disorder that causes children to have problems reading because they can't relate letters to words and identify speech sounds. This has also been called a reading disability. It can affect the area of the brain the helps us process language. A child who has dyslexia will have problems processing numbers and words. For example, Tommy works very hard at reading, but it never gets any easier. He realizes that he is smart but he just doesn't understand why he can't read as easy as the other children. Tommy has dyslexia.

Dyslexia is a learning disorder that some children have. It makes it hard for them to spell and read. This problem lives inside their brain but it does not mean they are dumb. A lot of talented and smart people have dyslexia. People who have dyslexia have normal vision and intelligence. Children who have dyslexia are able to do well in school with some specialized education or tutoring. Getting the right emotional support is also important.

Dyslexia is common and it makes it hard for them to read. Experts think that between five and ten percent of all people have it. Others think that it is more like 17 percent that show signs of having problems reading.

You can't outgrow dyslexia. There are strategies and ways to approach this problem that could help people who have dyslexia manage their challenges and improve their reading skills. It doesn't matter what age you are, you can be tested for dyslexia even though the tests will be different for children and adults.

There isn't a cure but early diagnosis and intervention can give the child a great outcome. There are times when dyslexia will go undiagnosed for many years and doesn't get noticed until the person is an adult. It isn't ever too late to get help.

How Reading Happens

In order to understand dyslexia better, you need to first know how reading happens. Reading can be a workout for the brain.

You have to do the following steps at one time:

1. Know how speech sounds to form words
2. Focus on the letters and words
3. Connect each letter with their speech sound

4. Smoothly blend all the letter sounds to make words

5. Control your eye movements as they move across the page

6. Create pictures and ideas

7. Compare all the new things with everything you already know

8. Store all these ideas into your memory.

Wow! That's a lot for a child who has dyslexia to struggle with. These are just the beginning steps and that means doing the remaining steps will be al lot harder. It isn't a surprise that learning to read and handling dyslexia makes a child's brain very tired more fast.

How a Child Learns to Read

Many children will learn to read by learning the way speech sounds create words. They will then connect all the sounds to the letters of the alphabet. They will learn that a "d" make a "duh" sound.

Then they will learn how to blend the sounds to make words. They will learn that a "d" and "og" make the word "dog." There will come a time when children won't have to sound out words and will be able to recognize a word that they have seen before.

This is a lot harder for children that have dyslexia. They are going to struggle just to remember the easy words that they have seen lots of times and sounding out long words. Why is this so hard for them?

Dyslexia means a child's brain has problems processing sounds and letters. It makes it hard to break words down into individual speech sounds like d-o-g for dog. If they have problems doing that, it will be extremely hard for them to connect speech sound to various letters like "duh" for "d," and to blend them into words they don't know yet.

A child with dyslexia is going to read slowly and they will make a lot of mistakes. They might mix up some letters at times in words like reading the word "saw" as the word "was." Words might be blended together wrong.

What Happens

Many children start learning how to read by figuring out how speech sounds are used in words and then they connect these sounds to letters of the alphabet. They will then learn ways to blend the sounds to form words and they will eventually recognize words that they have seen a lot of time.

Even before a child starts kindergarten, a child who has dyslexia might have trouble with sounds and letters. Their teacher might say they are smart but they seem to be struggling with learning to read. There might be times when a parent sees their child is struggling. The best thing a parent can do is to take them to a specialist who can help them figure out what is wrong.

Learning to read is like learning to ride a bike: it means you have to do many things at one time while using the right timing. With some practice, normal readers automatically learn how to read words slowly so they focus their mental energy on remembering and comprehending what they have just read.

Children who have dyslexia will have problems with phonics and phonemic awareness. Reading isn't automatic and will remain labored and slow. If a child struggles with these steps, comprehension will suffer and they will become frustrated.

One normal assumption about children with dyslexia is that words or letters look reversed such as the word "was" looks like "saw. This problem could be part of dyslexia but reversals are common with children until they are in second grade and not just with children who have dyslexia. The main problem for children who have dyslexia is rapid word recognition, phonics, and phonemic awareness.

A learning specialist will know a lot about learning issues that children have and things you can do for them. During a specialist's visit, a child might take a few tests. The main idea behind these tests isn't getting a good grade but to find problems. Finding a learning problem is the first step in getting the child the help that will help them learn easier.

Symptoms

Dyslexia can impact people in various ways. The symptoms may not look the same for everyone. The main sign for dyslexia is having problem decoding words. This is being able to match a letter to its correct sound. Children can struggle with the basic skill called phonemic awareness. This means they are able to recognize a word's sounds. Having problems with phonemic awareness could show up during preschool.

Dyslexia doesn't only affect learning. It could impact a child's daily activities and skills that include dealing with stress, memory, and social interactions.

The signs of dyslexia are hard to see before a child goes to school but there are some clues that could show they have problems. When your child goes to school, their teacher might be the first person to even notice they have a problem. How severe the disorder is will vary from child to child but the condition will become more apparent once the child begins reading.

☆ Before They Start School

Signs that a child might have dyslexia could include:

- Hard time playing rhyming games or learning nursery rhymes
- Problems remembering colors, numbers, and shapes
- Issues correctly forming words like confusing words that sound the same or reversing the sounds in words
- Slowly learning new words
- Talking later than other children of the same age
- Pronouncing long words
- Learning how to rhyme
- Learning the letters of the alphabet in the right sequence
- Learning the days of the week
- Learning to write and read their name
- Problems learning to figure out speech sounds and syllables in words
- Problems spelling and reading words using the right sequence of letters

- Fine motor and handwriting coordination

☆ Once They Go To School

After your child goes to school, dyslexia symptoms and signs might become more apparent and this includes:

- Avoiding any activity that involves reading

- Spending too much time finishing tasks that involve writing or reading

- Problems spelling

- Can't sound out words that they aren't familiar with

- Problems hearing or seeing differences or similarities in words and letters

- Problems remembering the order of things

- Problems forming the answer to questions or finding the right words

- Difficulty understanding and processing what they hear

- Reading below their age level

Adults and Teens

The signs of dyslexia in adults and teens are similar to ones in children. The common symptoms and signs in adults and teens include:

☆ Problems figuring out math word problems

☆ Spelling and reading below their grade level

☆ Problems memorizing things

☆ Difficulty learning new languages

☆ Problems retelling a story

☆ Taking a long time finishing tasks that involve writing or reading

☆ Problems understanding expressions or jokes that have meanings that aren't easily understood from a certain word like the phrase "piece of cake" means "easy"

☆ Problems pronouncing words or names or they can't retrieve a word from their memory

☆ Staying away from any activity that involves reading

☆ Difficulty spelling

☆ Has a hard time writing and reading

☆ Problems reading especially out loud

When to Go to Your Doctor

Even though most children are eager and ready to learn how to read by the time they go to kindergarten, if a child has dyslexia they can't understand reading basics by that time. You need to talk with their doctor if your child isn't interested in reading or is slower than what is expected for their age or if you see other signs that they might have dyslexia.

If dyslexia doesn't get diagnosed and it goes untreated, their reading problems will continue for the rest of their lives.

Diagnosing

Dyslexia normally gets diagnosed while the child is still in elementary school. There might be times when it doesn't show up until the child gets older and they are expected to read and comprehend more complex materials. Constantly having problems with advanced spelling, reading or learning a new language could be signs that a teenager might have dyslexia.

The only way dyslexia can be diagnosed is by a comprehensive evaluation by a psychologist or a reading specialist. Pediatricians usually know some signs of dyslexia and can help the family find the right help for their child.

If there are delays in identifying dyslexia could cause larger problems and could cause low self esteem. It is important that you recognize the symptoms early in the child's life and begin specialized programs to help your child immediately.

Getting the correct diagnosis could lead to services and support at school and accommodations when at work or college.

There are several professionals that can test people for dyslexia. These are neuropsychologists, clinical psychologists, and school psychologists. They will give the person several tests specialized for dyslexia. They will test in other areas to see where any strengths or weaknesses might be.

Being evaluated at school is always free. Private evaluations could be costly. There are some cases where a family can get at a lower cost or possibly free. Some local universities normally have some psychology programs that will have a clinic where a student can do their training.

Hospitals that teach might have some research projects where people can be evaluated for free. LDA or the Learning Disabilities Association of America has local chapter in all states. They could help you find low cost or free options.

Causes

Scientists haven't found the exact cause of dyslexia. They know that brain differences and genes do have a role.

1. Heredity and Genes

Dyslexia isn't a disease. It is something that somebody is born with and it normally runs in families. Around 40 percent of the people who have dyslexia will have siblings that have problems reading, too. There is about 49 percent of all parents who have a child that was diagnosed with dyslexia will have dyslexia, too. It is linked to a specific gene that affects how the brain processes language and reading along with other risk factors in their environment. Children who have dyslexia aren't lazy or stupid. Most will have an average intelligence some might have an above average intelligence and they work extremely hard learning how to overcome their learning disability.

2. Brain Activity and Anatomy

Images of the brain have shown that there are differences between people who do and don't have dyslexia. The differences show up in the areas that are involved with main reading skills. Skills like knowing how sounds are shown in words and seeing what a written word should look like.

Research shows that dyslexia happens because of the way our brains process information. When pictures of the brain are taken when dyslexic people read, it shows that different parts of the brain are used than in people who don't have dyslexia. This showed the brain of people who have dyslexia doesn't work right when they read. This is why reading is so hard for them.

Brains do have the ability to change. Studies have shown that brain activity in people who have dyslexia can change after they get the right kind of tutoring and instruction. Scientists are still learning more about it, too.

Risk Factors

There are several risk factors of dyslexia, and they include:

- ☆ Problems in the areas of the brain that help with reading

- ☆ Exposure to infections, alcohol, drugs, and nicotine while pregnant can change the fetus' brain development

- ☆ Low birth weight or premature birth

- ☆ Family history of learning disabilities or dyslexia

Complications

Dyslexia could lead to several problems, and these include:

☆ Problems in Adulthood

Not being able to read and comprehend what they read could keep a child from reaching their full potential as the child gets older. This could have some severe economic, social, and educational consequences.

☆ Social Problems

If dyslexia isn't treated, it could lead to withdrawal from teachers, parents, and friends, aggression, anxiety, behavioral problems, and low self-esteem.

☆ Learning Problems

Since reading is a basic skill that is needed for most school subjects, a child who has dyslexia has a disadvantage in many classes and might have problems keeping up in class.

Children that have dyslexia have more of a risk of developing ADHD or attention deficit hyperactivity disorder. ADHD could cause problems with a child keeping their attention on a task, and this could lead to dyslexia, too. This can cause dyslexia harder to treat.

Managing Dyslexia

With the right help and assistance, many children who have dyslexia can learn to read and create strategies that help them remain in their normal classroom.

They normally work with a reading specialist, tutors, specially trained teacher that can help them learn how to spell, read, and manage their dyslexia. Your child's pediatrician, psychologist, or teacher might recommend a therapist known as either an academic language therapist or an education therapist. These people have been trained to work with children who have dyslexia.

Within the United States, federal laws give children with language based or reading problems special help in public schools like extra time doing homework, taking tests, help taking notes, and specialized instructions. Each state has its own laws in place for this type of help. Parents need to talk about these accommodations and laws with their staff.

Making It Easier for Them

Many children who have dyslexia are able to learn to read with the right type of teaching. They may learn a way that helps them remember sounds. The letters "p" and "b" are brother sounds because they are both called "lip poppers." You need to press your lips together in order to make their sounds.

Thinking about how our mouths move in order to make a sound could help a child learn to read easier. Learning specialists know many activities that can help a child who has dyslexia learn how to read.

Children can use flash cards, tape their homework assignments, and lessons rather than trying to take notes by themselves. They might need their tutors or parents to help them remain caught up.

Getting extra time on tests is extremely important. Children who have dyslexia need to have enough time to finish the test and show their teacher just what they have learned. Computers can help, too. There are programs that will "read" a book out loud to the child. You can even download books onto an iPod.

How Children Feel

Children with dyslexia might get frustrated, sad, or angry because spelling and reading are so hard. They might not like having to go see a special tutor or being in different reading groups than the other children.

Getting help is very important, and it will give them a boost to help them continue learning to read. Before they realize it, they have gone on to do wonderful things in their lives. Some of the most successful and creative people have dyslexia. Dyslexia didn't stop them from pursuing their dreams.

Other Things to Know

Children who have dyslexia might feel like they aren't as smart as the other children in their class because it is hard for them to keep up. As they go through elementary school, their problems could get worse as reading will become more important to their learning.

Children who have problems usually stay away from reading since it is stressful and hard. This means that they miss out on reading practice and they fall farther and farther behind their peers.

It is very important to support your child's efforts by helping and encouraging them when they read at home. Try to give them as many opportunities as you can to help build their confidence so they can be successful in other areas like drama, arts, hobbies, and sports. Statesmen, lawyers, doctors, entrepreneurs, scientists, athletes, and artists have been able to reach their goals and achieve great things in spite of their problems with reading.

If you suspect your child has dyslexia, talk with their doctor, reading specialist, or teacher as soon as you can. The sooner you can find their problem, the sooner you can give them the right help.

Give Them a Reason to Read

A child with dyslexia will do whatever they can to avoid reading because it is difficult for them. The problem here is, you need to make sure that they are reading so that they don't have to worry about learning the skills later in life. Reading and writing skills are very important to everybody because it is something we will use our entire life. So, the first step in helping your child is to give them some incentive to get them reading. The best way to do this is through a token economy.

A token economy is simply a type of behavior modification that is designed to increase certain behaviors and to decrease other types of behaviors through the use of tokens. A person will receive tokens immediately after they have performed the desirable behavior. They are able to collect the tokens and then get to exchange them in for a privilege or meaningful object later on.

This is something that a lot of grade school teachers use, and you may have used a system like this at some point in their life already, such as potty training. If your child gets an allowance for doing chores around the house is the same concept.

The primary goal of a token economy is to get your child to do more things that you want them to do. In this case, it would be reading, writing, homework, or anything else they avoid due to their dyslexia. Also, you want to decrease their avoidance of those things. Token economies are often used in institutional settings to help manage the behaviors of individuals who are prone to unpredictable and aggressive actions. However, the larger goal of the token economy is to help teach appropriate actions and social skills that will help a person in their natural environment. Token economies also work in group settings as well.

Setting Up a Token Economy

There are a few different things you need to create a token economy.

1. Tokens

Anything that can be seen and counted can become a token. You want the tokens to be something attractive, difficult to copy, and easy to carry and use. Some of the most commonly used items are play money, point tallies, stickers, or poker chips. When your child does something that you want them to, they should be immediately given a certain number of tokens.

Tokens don't have any actual value on their own. They have saved up and then later exchanged for activities, meaningful objects, and privileges. It is possible for your child to lose tokens if they act in a way that you don't want them to.

If you think about it, tokens are just like money. In the world, people go to work, do their job, and get money to spend on things that you need or want. This is pretty much identical to a token economy. The money that you earn at your work isn't really the things you want. What you really want is to buy that car, house, vacation, groceries, what have you. With the token economy, your child goes to school, does what they are supposed to, and earns tokens to spend on things they want. Again, the tokens aren't what they want. They are simply a means to an end.

2. Defined Target behavior

Your child needs to know exactly what they have to do in order to earn a token. Undesirable and desirable behaviors have to be explained to them ahead of time in specific and simple terms. You should also specify how many tokens they will get or lose for each type of behavior.

3. Back-up Reinforcers

These reinforcers are the activities, meaningful objects, and privileges that individuals get when they exchange their tokens. These reinforcers could be outings, extra free times, toys, or food items. The success of this system will depend greatly on the appeal of these back-up reinforcers. Your child is only going to be motivated to earn their tokens if they can anticipate the future reward that the tokens represent. A well-designed token economy will use back-up reinforcers that are picked out by your child rather than you.

4. System for Token Exchange

You have to come up with a time and place for the purchasing of the back-up reinforcers. You will have predetermined the token value of these back-up reinforcers based on their value to your child. For example, if the reinforcement is very attractive or expensive, then its token value needs to be higher. If the item could help your child out in some way, then the value would be lower. If you set the token value too low, your child won't be as motivated to earn more tokens. Conversely, if you place the value too high, then your child can end up becoming discouraged.

5. System to Record Data

Before your token economy begins, you should have some sort of baseline reading for your child. This tends to be more for your use than your child's so that you know the token economy is working. The baseline would basically be how well your child is doing in school or how often they read, and other the things they have been struggling with. Then, you can update this information in the coming weeks or months to have you establish the token economy. You should also record the exchange of the tokens.

6. Consistent Implementation

If you want the token economy to succeed, everybody involved has to reward the same actions, use the correct amount of tokens, avoid giving away back-up reinforcers, and prevent fake tokens from being made, stolen, or unjustly obtained. This means that you and your significant other should know the exact rules for the system, and both of you should follow it.

What Should Tokens Be?

Using the word token makes you think of something physical that you can easily hold. There are some token economies that will use physical objects. Some systems will use physical objects like marbles, fake money, cards with smiley aces, or poker chips. However, you don't know have to use physical items. Some will have a paper with tick marks; a hole punched card, or a stamp on a card. The only issue with the non-physical options is that they can't be easily taken away if your child loses some, except for tick marks which can be erased.

Starting Your Token Economy

When you first start using the token economy, tokens should be awarded more frequently and in larger amounts, but as your child learns the desirable actions, their opportunities to earn tokens should decrease. For example, on the first day, you could give them 25 to 75 tokens for reading, doing their homework, or doing something that you would like them to do so that they learn the tokens value. Later on, you may only allow them to earn 15 to 30 tokens during a day. As you gradually start decreasing the availability of tokens, your child should learn to perform the desired actions without the need for a token. Reinforcers that your child would experience in society, such as verbal praise, need to accompany the awarding of tokens to help with the process of fading.

The advantage of using a token economy is that behaviors can be rewarded immediately and the punishment of losing tokens is less restrictive than other types of punishments, and your child is able to learn skills that they are going to need in the future.

The best thing you can do to get your token economy on its feet is to sit down with your child and discuss it with them. This way, you can make sure the backup reinforcers are something they want and that you are both on the same page as to what they need to do to earn their tokens. You can also meet back up from time to time to change things around if need be.

Token Economy Chart

Token economies for children tend to use a chart. There is not a single type of chart that has to be used, and you can make yours; however, you would like. There are some that have a large box with the image of what your child is working towards, the reinforce, on the top. Then there are others that have space for you to write down different things that are being earned, and then there are some that simply have space for you to record how many tokens they have earned.

For charts that don't display one single reinforcer, there will typically be some type of method for your child to choose from a group of reinforcers once they have filled the chart or you can create a list of reinforcers that "cost" different amounts, and it will be up to your child what they choose to trade in their tokens for.

Token Economy Example

To give you an idea of how a token economy works, let's look at an example of one. For this example, the parent and their child, Steve, has talked about what is going on, and Steve understands that the goal is for him to read more.

The target behavior is for Steve to read for at least 30 minutes each day. These 30 minutes do not have to be in a row, and he is free to ask for help with the reading. The important thing is that he makes an effort to read.

The tokens he is given are raffle tickets that they get each time they reach their goal.

The backup reinforcers is an extra 30 minutes of free time that Steve gets to choose what he wants to do.

At the end of the day, Steve will receive five tokens if they have read for at least 30 minutes during the day

Steve has to earn 50 tokens to get 30 minutes of free time. This means, if he reaches his goal 10 days in a row, he will get the backup reinforcer.

The time and place to exchange his tokens in for his backup reinforcer are done on Friday evenings so that he can use his reinforcement during the weekend. As you can see, this is a simple version of the token economy, and only one backup reinforce is involved. You can feel free to have as many backup reinforcers as you want, and it is best to have multiple target behaviors that your child can perform to earn tokens.

Response Cost

We've mentioned, in passing, that your child could lose token if they engage in behaviors you don't want them to exhibit. In larger settings with bigger stakes, such as psychiatric hospitals or prison, response costs are more important because they tend to engage in very undesirable actions. When it comes to your child, response costs should only be used for major undesirable actions that tend to call attention to themselves and should be suppressed. Your primary attention should always be tuned into the positive behaviors that you want to reinforce. Response cost should always be a last resort and should be combined with other things to help your child build adaptive behaviors. Your job as a parent is hard, and as such, you wouldn't want to take tokens away from your child for an innocent accident simply because you were in a bad mood.

This is why it helps to define the actions that would cause a response cost when you define the target behavior. This will prevent you from taking away tokens when it isn't necessary.

A response cost is simply a fine where you remove tokens your child has earned, much like you would have to pay a fine if you were caught speeding. It is very important that your child understands what actions will cost them tokens. It's not far if they don't actually know the rules. You should also never place your child in a token debt. At that point, you are going to be doing more harm than good for your child.

Conditioned Reinforcement

The token economy is a type of conditioned reinforcement or "secondary reinforcement."

This is because the tokens your child earns are not naturally occurring reinforcers. The natural reinforcers in your child's like, like water and food, would be called unconditioned reinforcers or "primary reinforcers" because they don't have to be paired with other things.

The money you get for going to work is a type of conditioned reinforcement because money is not a natural reinforcement. Look at it this way. Imagine that when you go into work, you are given some plastic chips at the end of the workday. It is very unlikely that you will be happy about those chips. However, if you were told that you can trade in those chips for an extra vacation day, the chips are going to become something that you will want to earn more of.

This causes those chips to become conditioned reinforcers because they have been paired the chance to take a day off from work. When it comes to children, the tokens are a way for them to get access to preferred items and activities.

Risks

A token economy can come with some risks, and these risks tend to vary between settings. For example, token economies used in a rehabilitation system can run the risk of staff members not being on the same page and neglecting the patient in the long run. But, since you will be using one in your home for your child, then you should run into the same risks. The biggest risk for parents is if they have multiple children, and the other feel left out. It's important that you establish a token economy for all of your children in some way so that you don't cause a rift between your kids.

Another issue can be that parents may forget that their child needs to be given the same type of encouragement and attention that they would normally get without the token economy. Just because you are rewarding certain behaviors with tokens does not mean that you should tell them what a good job they did on something else. Treat your children like you always have with the addition of the token economy.

Like we talked about in the last point, a token economy is a conditional reinforcement. They have to earn tokens. But, your love, affection, and attention should still be unconditional. The token economy does not change that.

If you sign up at this link https://forms.gle/wXHrfS5G8Vj47bMX8 I'll send you some important tools to realize your token economy.

#3

Emotional Support

Most learning disabilities come with hidden costs, and dyslexia is no exception. A child with dyslexia likely feels embarrassed or frustrated whenever they are asked to do things like reading out loud because they are difficult tasks. This is especially true when they are in class, or other students are around. The problems go beyond school, though. The impact dyslexia can have on day-to-day activities, such as play board games and following directions, or even reading the clock accurately, can cause a child to feel avoidant and self-conscious.

Helping them to understand their learning disorder can provide them with the tools that they need to manage their dyslexia, both emotionally and academically. Not every dyslexic person will experience discouragement, and all that comes along with it, however, most families will experience a couple of issues.

Some kids will have trouble in social situations. They may be socially and emotionally immature, which can affect the relationships they have, which will end up causing a lack of confidence.

Processing lags will often cause a dyslexic child to have a hard time finding the right words or to keep up with conversations in a group setting. This becomes more prevalent once they reach their teen years.

All of this adds and can cause increased fear of embarrassment and failure, and anxiety. Anxiety will cause them to want to avoid situations that could be awkward, which will end up causing more criticism from the unknowing teachers and parents.

All of this frustration can end up causing anger, which may make the child appear that they are being rebellious. Understanding the root of the issue is very important for the parents. Nobody knows your child like you do. The majority of dyslexic children who go to public schools end up waiting for the school to help them learn, and they end up falling further and further behind. The daily comparison to kids who are able to learn through traditional means can easily break apart their confidence.

There are some kids with dyslexia who can brush off their struggles and press through cheerfully while others end up experiencing:

☆ Loss of Confidence

During their early years, a child spends this time developing their self-image. If these years are filled with frustrations from school, they can end up turning into feelings of inferiority. If they do not receive help for this, it can end up causing them to feel incompetent and powerless.

Research has found that these feelings of inferiority develop by age ten. After this point, it becomes very hard to help a child develop a positive self-image. This is a very strong argument for early intervention.

☆ Depression

These same frustrations can end up causing some children to become depressed. The most common signs of depression in children can be very different than the signs in adults. Signs of depression in kids can include negative thoughts about themselves; they lack hope or the ability to imagine a positive future, and views the world negatively.

☆ Family Problems

Interestingly, sibling rivalry is very common in homes with one or more dyslexic children. Children without dyslexia end up feeling jealous of the attention, money, and time that is spent on the dyslexic child. This negative attention is unwanted by the dyslexic child and creates more stress.

Parents can end up misunderstanding dyslexia and will insist that their child simply needs to work harder, which does nothing. If the parent has dyslexia as well, watching their child have to go through all of the same struggles can cause them a lot of pain that can stir up bad memories.

☆ No Interest in Learning

If a child constantly performs below expectations and no matter how hard they work, they still fall short, it is very easy to understand why they lose interest in learning.

☆ Low Patience with Difficult

Without having any regular success, those with dyslexia can develop a lower tolerance for difficulty, which can cause them to give up quickly if they think something is too hard.
It's tough for a child who is bright but constantly falls short in school. But with a little help for you, they can overcome these side effects of dyslexia.

Overcoming Emotional Issues

What will determine if a person with dyslexia thrives or not is having somebody present in their life that is encouraging and supportive. As the parent reading this, then that is likely you. Know that through your advocacy and support can be the most effective thing you can do for them, whether or not you end up making mistakes. Let's look at some things you can do to help your child to make sure they don't develop these emotional side effects.

☆ Education

Teachers are just as guilty of not understanding dyslexia. This means you, as the parent, need to make sure your child and their teacher know what dyslexia is and is not. Help your child to understand that they truly are smart; they simply learn in a different way. They may benefit from a dyslexia course. These courses go into detail about all of the different aspects of dyslexia and focus on the strengths of the dyslexic mind which tend to get overlooked.

☆ Self-Advocacy

This works with education. A dyslexic child who is able to understand their diagnosis is able to be taught to advocate for themselves. This means that they will be able to tell their friend, Scout leader, or teacher what their needs are upfront and won't have to wait until a situation ends up getting out of control before starting the conversation.

☆ Find Their Strengths

Figure out what areas your child naturally succeeds, whether it is athletics, mechanical, arts, or whatever. Use those strengths to help them learn and to boost their confidence.

☆ Take a Break

Studies have found that those who are anxious can't learn. If your child is feeling anxious about schoolwork, it could be best if you back off on the academics for a bit. At school, they may not be able to take a break, but at home, you should give them a break so that their brain has a chance to rest. If you homeschool your child, then you have the freedom to give them a break whenever they need to.

Taking a break does not mean that they stop learning. Sometimes those breaks should mean you move away from the books and head outside for some real life learning. You can go to a museum, beach, or whatever your child likes. Use these adventures and chances to learn. Show them how learning can be rewarding and fun.

☆ Listen To How They Feel

Listen to what your kid and hear what they say about their feelings. Remember, there are some dyslexic kids who have processing and speech lags, so make sure you are quick to listen and slow to speak.

The most important thing for you to do is make sure that you are there for them. However, they need you. This could mean simply being there to listen to their struggles or to help them with their homework. Provide them the support they need so that they don't feel like they are going through this alone.

#4

Set Routines

Why does a child with dyslexia need routines? Routines help children create self-discipline and give them a sense of security.

Humans have a fear of many things, but "the unknown" is above everything else except public speaking and death for many.

When children are afraid of the unknown, this might include everything from major changes in their lives or being introduced to a new veggie. Children get confronted with change on a daily basis. This can help them grow but it can be stressful, too.

When a child grows up, their bodies are changing on them all the time. Toddlers and babies learn to give up breasts, bottles, pacifiers, cribs, and them being a baby. New classmates and teachers will come and go each year. They learn new information and skills quickly. This could be anything from riding a bike, soccer, crossing the street, and reading. Not all children will live in the same exact house throughout their whole childhood but many will move several times.

Sometimes they will move to new schools, neighborhoods, and cities.

Most of these changes aren't within their control.

Children handle change the best if it happens within their control. A routine lets a child feel safe enough to create a sense of mastery when being able to handle their lives. When this sense of mastery gets strengthened, they will be able to tackle bigger changes like going to camp, paying for their own things, or walking to school alone.

What happens if they are faced with an unpredictable change like their mom gets called away on a business trip, or their best friend moves to a new school? If it is something extremely drastic like their grandparent died or their parents are getting divorced. This can remove their sense of mastery and safety and leave them feeling anxious and unable to deal with life. Most changes can't be avoided but this is why we give children a routine as a concrete foundation in their lives. This helps them rise above the occasion to be able to hand changes when needed.

When you can help your children feel ready and safe to take on new developmental tasks and challenges, you are giving them structure. This has other important roles, too. Routines can teach a child ways to manage their environments and themselves.

Children who live in chaotic homes where their things aren't ever out away won't learn that life can run smoother if you are more organized. If they live in homes where there isn't a set space or time to do homework, children won't learn how to sit down and tackle unpleasant and sometimes impossible tasks, especially if they are dyslexic. Children who don't learn how to take care of themselves like brushing their teeth, brushing their hair, showering, learning how to make a sandwich, or fixing a bowl of cereal might find it difficult to take care of themselves when they become young adults. Having structure lets us learn good habits.

Routines are the way families get organized in order to have fun, spend time together, and get things done. Each family is going to have its own unique routine. These can help the members of the family know who has to do what, how often, in what order, and when to do it.

You family may have:

- ☆ Daily routines for mornings, work, bath time, greetings, goodbyes, meals, bath time, and bedtime.

- ☆ Weekly routines for cleaning, washing, and other housework

- ☆ Other routines for get-togethers and holidays.

Family life can be smoother when it has some routines. There is a lot more to routines than just this. Routines let your children know what is important. Special routines sometimes referred to as a ritual, can help strengthen your values and beliefs. They can help build a sense of togetherness and belonging to your family life.

Dulling Creativity and Spontaneity

Will too much structure dull a child's sense of creativity and spontaneity? If it is imposed without sensitivity, there will be times when rules can be broken like leaving the dishes in the sink in order to play charades with the family or letting the child stay up late to see a lunar eclipse. The most creative artists begin by mastering their past and finding ways to be creative while working within certain rules.

There isn't any reason why structure needs to oppress anyone. You need to think of it as your best friend. It offers you traditions and routines that make life cozier and easier. Your children will soak up this security, but they will be able to structure their lives.

Should Infants Have Routines

Absolutely not! Infants will always tell us what they are in need of. They get fed when they are hungry. We change them when they are wet. With time, they will learn this as a routine. At night, we sleep. We can't force an infant to adhere to our routine because we aren't responsive to their needs. They aren't capable of adapting to our routine just yet. If their needs aren't met, they are going to feel like their world is a place where their needs aren't ever met so they have to be dramatic to get them met.

Once your infant moves into being a crawler, they will establish their own routine by creating their own schedule. Most babies will settle into a pattern that is fairly predictable. You can help them by structuring your day around what they need. Make sure the conditions are right for their nap time. With time, you can respond to their natural schedule of sleeping and eating by creating a routine that works for the entire family.

Benefits of Routines

Children who have dyslexia need and like having routines. Routines, in general, have some benefits for your child.

1. Belonging and Safety

A predictable and organized home can help children of all ages feel safe, looked after, and secure, especially during stressful or difficult times of their lives such as puberty.

Routines that are built around spending time together and having fun can strengthen the family's relationships. Reading a story before bedtime, having a special snack after soccer practice could turn into a special time for you to share with your child.

2. Gets Rid of Power Struggles

When you create a routine, it will get rid of any power struggle since you won't be bossing you child. Whatever activity they need to do like turning off the television, taking a nap, brushing their teeth, etc. is just things you do a certain time throughout the day. You stop being a bad guy, and all the nagging is reduced.

3. Responsibility and Skills

Having chores can help children with or without dyslexia and of all ages develop responsibility and basic skills such as managing time. These are skills that they will be able to take with them throughout their lives.

Once a child learns to do their part without supervision from you, it can help them become independent.

4. Help Kids Learn About Cooperation

Routines will help kids learn to cooperate by reducing anxiety and stress on everybody. Everyone will know what will come next because they get a transition warning and nobody will feel like they are being pushed around.

5. Healthy Habits

Routines can help teach your young children some healthy habits such as washing their hands after going to the bathroom, getting exercise, taking their medicines, and brushing their teeth.

This means that routines are good for your child's health. Children that wash their hands regularly won't get as many colds or other illnesses. Routines can lower stress, which is good for a child's immune system.

Routines can help set our body clocks. Bedtime routines can help a child's body "know" when it is time to go to sleep. This could help when a child reaches adolescence, and their body's clocks begin changing.

6. Helps Children Take Charge of Their Activities

With time, children are going to learn how to pack their own backpacks and brush their teeth without being reminded. Children love to be in charge of themselves. This can increase their sense of competence and mastery. Children who feel in charge of themselves and independent will have no need to be oppositional or rebel against you.

7. Learn to Look Forward to What they Like

Looking forward to getting to do the things they enjoy is important to make your family feel accommodated even while staying on a schedule. They might want to go to the park right now, but they will be able to learn that they get to go to the park after their nap or lunch and then they get to look forward to that.

8. Keeps Children Stay on Schedule

Normal routines can help a child get on and stay on schedule so they can fall asleep easily.

9. Helps Parents Build Connections

Everyone knows that we have to connect with our children daily. If we only focus on moving children through a schedule, we are going to miss out on all the opportunities we have to make a connection to our children. If you can build a ritual into the routine, they turn into habits. Try snuggling with your child when you see them first thing in the morning.

You could also have a recognition ritual every time you see them: "I see you with those beautiful blue eyes that I love." You could do a name game as you dry them off after their bath: "Let's dry your toes... your feet... your calf... your knees... your thighs... your belly..." These rituals might slow you down some, but they can connect you on a deeper level. If you do them as a routine, they are going to build security, cooperation, and connections.

10. Helps You Keep Expectations

If you are constantly fighting with your child, you are just going to settle. You begin letting them skip brushing their teeth. You let them watch an hour more television. When you have a routine, you will stick with the healthier expectations for all members of the family since this is the way our family does things. You will end up with the result that a family who has healthy habits lives in a house where everything runs smoother.

Why Routines Are Good for Parents

Routines take time and effort to create. When you have them set up, they can have a lot of benefits:

- ☆ Routines can free you up from making decisions and resolving fights. If you have pizza every Sunday, nobody will need to argue about what you are having for dinner.

- ☆ If life is busy, routines could help you feel like you are in control and organized, and this can lower your stress.

- ☆ Consistent and regular routines could help you feel like you are being a good parent.

- ☆ Routings can help you do your daily tasks, and this gives you free time to do the things you love.

What Is a Good Routine?

There aren't any rules about what type or how many routines you need to have. Every family is different, and what works for one may not work for others. Your routine needs to be based on your family's needs. Effective routines will have three main features:

☆ Predictable: in good routines, things are going to happen in the exact same order every time. You do the laundry every weekend, so the child will know they have clean clothes on Monday.

☆ Regular: Good routines will become a part of your daily family life. You might go to grandma's house each Sunday for a family barbecue.

Well planned: Good routines will make sure everybody knows what they have to do, and they will view their role as fair and reasonable. Your child will know that they have to take turns washing and drying the dishes after dinner each night.

Ideas for Toddler and Preschool Routines

For children who are fairly young, you could help them learn routines for:

☆ Eating meals

☆ Getting up each morning and getting ready for preschool

☆ Playing with others at the park

☆ Spending time talking and playing daily

☆ Telling stories or reading

☆ Having quiet time before going to bed

☆ Brushing their teeth

☆ Changing their clothes

☆ Good night kiss

Ideas for School-age Children Routines

For children who are old enough to go to school, you could make routines for:

☆ Getting up and getting dressed each morning

☆ Picking up their toys

☆ Playing with other children after school or a few times each week

☆ Giving them tokens to buy rewards at the end of the week

- ☆ Being active in sports or hobbies

- ☆ Setting the table at mealtime, unloading the dishwasher, folding the laundry, feeding the pet.

Ideas for Teenager Routines

Teenagers and older children may grow out of or begin challenging some of their routines. You are going to need to be flexible and change their routine as they get older. You may need to change a child's bedtime routine or their chores they do so they stay challenged.

For teenagers, you could create a routine:

- ☆ Participating in activities after school like sports or hobbies

- ☆ Making sure they do their homework

- ☆ Cleaning their room

- ☆ Making their bed

- ☆ Helping with the laundry

- ☆ Helping with the dishes

Ideas for The Whole Family Routines

To keep the family involved with each other, you could create some routines like:

☆ Participating in community activities

☆ Participating in celebrations

☆ Visiting extended family

☆ Visiting sick friends

☆ Spending one on one time with parents

☆ Taking turn talking during dinner

☆ Have a family meeting

☆ Taking walks after dinner

☆ Having a movie night

☆ Eating meals together

#5

Read With Them

A lot of parents of dyslexic children experience frustration when it comes to trying to get them to read. It makes sense that a dyslexic child doesn't want to read. Who would want to spend time doing something that is hard? Nobody. But, parents also understand that reading is a very important way to acquire knowledge. Reading is also a great way to enhance your vocabulary. Both of these things are critical to learning, especially when it comes to the school curriculum.

We also understand that the more a person reads, the better reader they are going to become, and the more knowledge they will accrue. Research has proven that dyslexic children are at risk of not acquiring the knowledge they need simply because they don't read as much as their peers. Then, weak reading skills coupled with repeated failures, cause children to read even less. This will only cause more difficulties. This means that parents and educators are faced with a conundrum. How can we ensure that children with dyslexia can access the same texts as their when their reading levels don't allow them to.

This can be done by having your child listen to what they're reading

There are a few different ways to do this. One way is to simply read them a book as they follow along; another way is to have them listen to audiobooks while following along. Audiobooks are actually very powerful tools that can improve your child's comprehension, improve their confidence, save some time on schoolwork, and help them earn better grades.

When your child listens to an audiobook as they follow along with the text, it can help them to bridge the gap between decoding words and assigning them meaning. When they receive information both audibly and visually, it helps to reinforce their word recognition, builds vocabulary, improves fluency, and supports the development of their comprehension skills.

As your child progresses in school, keeping up with the ever increasing amounts of reading can be hard for them. Audiobooks are able to help them by giving them the chance to focus on the meaning of what they are reading instead of having to decode all of the words on the page. In general, your child's listening comprehension is likely going to be stronger than their reading comprehension. When they listen to text, they are able to access content that might have been above their current reading levels, which makes learning new information easier.

Audiobooks are also able to help ease frustrations, boost confidence, and make reading more enjoyable for dyslexic children. They also help children learn to enjoy literature and build a diverse and wide knowledge base. This is very important to unlocking the magical world of stories for them so that they are able to experience getting lost in a book just like other kids.

Besides, audiobooks, you can also use text-to-speech technology. This can open them up to a vast number of opportunities for acquiring knowledge. First, it will allow them to enjoy books that match up with their spoken language comprehension level. People with dyslexia often have an average or above average receptive language skills. Students need to be able to access grade-level or higher texts in order to support their continued development of language skills. Having a wide and rich exposure to books and readings will help to promote the growth of literate language forms, complex syntactic forms, and new vocabulary, and this exposure will help to improve a student's understanding and knowledge of the world. When you encourage a student to read a large variety of different texts, it will improve their knowledge of different types of text structures that they may come across.

Plus, using text-to-speech technology will allow your children to read books that they find interesting no matter what skill level they are. If your child is able to read materials that interest them, they are going to be more likely to continue to engage in reading for the fun of it. There is research that has found that successful adults who have dyslexic learned better when they started pursuing topics that interested them. By choosing a topic of interested, it gave them the motivation to conquer, tackle, and persevere their biggest enemy, which is reading. This meant that they learned related concepts and vocabulary and built a greater understanding of the context. There were some whose topics of interest turned out to be a lifelong hobby. For others, their topic of interest that inspired them to read was related to their future career.

Children with dyslexia shouldn't just read with their ears or "read with their ears." Instead, text-to-speech software or audiobooks should be used as an accommodation. There are some who view the use of audiobooks like cheating, like it isn't a legitimate way to read. This isn't true. It is common for people with dyslexia and other reading disorders to listen to text. It's not even noticeable or unusual even more to hear or see people listening to books. Using text-to-speech support helps to level the playing field for those with dyslexia so that they are able to have the same opportunities as everyone else. It is always best to use technology that gives your child the ability to track the print as they hear the book being read. With that said, it is okay if they simply enjoy listening to a book from time to time.

That being said, let's go over a few websites where you can find some free audiobooks for your child to enjoy.

Bookshare

Bookshare is one of the leading sources for free digital text-to-speech books. It has one of the largest online libraries of accessible reading materials. Through this site, your child will be able to read children's classics as well as textbooks. They will also have access to current magazines and bestsellers. When your child is a member, they will be able to access as many books as they want to. Bookshare can be used on a Chromebook or a computer, or you can get it on a tablet using Voice Dream Reader, Go Read for Android phones, and Read2Go on iOS.

In order to sign up for Bookshare, you will have to show that your child has a disability that hinders their ability to read traditional print books. Students who have learning difficulties, like dyslexia, could qualify. You can have your child evaluated in order to get the documentation to prove their dyslexia.

Bookshare is free for all US students who qualify. This also includes college students and adult education programs. For people who do not qualify, it costs $50 each year along with a one-time $25 setup fee. Bookshare gets its funding from the US Department of Education.

Local Libraries and Schools

Another great place to get free audiobooks and text-to-speech books is through your local library and at your child's school. Library audiobooks are not normally synced up to the text, so this means that your child will listen as they follow along in a regular printed book.

Libraries and schools sometimes provide free text-to-speech books to students. There are some schools that will actually give your child a membership to Bookshare if they have an IEP or a 504 plan for reading issues. Talk to the staff at your child's school or a librarian about the types of programs that they may have for them.

Online Help

There are many different types of websites that provide access to digital books and audiobooks. These won't need you to prove that your child suffers from a reading problem, but their selections tend to be limited to older classics. The following are some good sites to try:

☆ Storynory

This website offers free audiobooks to young children. They will have access to fairy tales like *Little Red Riding Hood*, as well as other classics like *Alice in Wonderland*. Every audiobook has its own digital text for the book.

☆ Lit2Go

You can find free audiobooks on the site of books that are no longer protected by copyright law. LibriVox is another site that offers a similar service. Lit2Go has downloadable PDFs of the books so that they will be able to read along as they listen to classic stories like *The Call of the Wild*. The site also helps out by categorizing the books by reading level.

☆ Project Gutenberg

One last option is Project Gutenberg. While you aren't going to find any recent bestsellers, they do have over 50,000 free classic books in digital form. Most of the digital books will be able to be read with text-to-speech. In order to have these books read aloud, your child will need to download the free digital book onto a mobile device or computer. Then they will be able to use text-to-speech technology to listen to the book. You can download the books from Project Gutenberg straight onto the Voice Dream Reader app.

Difference Between Audiobooks and Text-to-Speech

It is important to understand that there are some slight differences between audiobooks and text-to-speech technology. While they will both help your child read, they do have different qualities that could affect which one your child would prefer.

First, an audiobook is an audio recording of a book where somebody is reading it aloud. Text-to-speech is a technology that will speak aloud digital text, like books, magazines, news articles, and websites.

Audiobooks have human voices, which makes them easy to understand and sometimes more entertaining because of the voice actor. This will add to the story and will help with the understanding of the book because of its changes in tone and emotions. There will also be natural pauses. The text-to-speech will be a computer-generated voice. There is a lot of different TTS software out there. As technology starts to improve, the voice will become more natural. Since it is not a human voice, the reading can be a bit difficult to understand. It may pronounce words wrong. The pauses will likely not make sense. There won't be any reaction in tone or emotions.

The one thing that TTS software often does is highlight the words as it reads it, whereas audiobooks don't typically do that. The prices vary a lot as well. Audiobooks tend to be very inexpensive, and you can even find some for free. Libraries carry them as well. TTS software sometimes com built into phones, tables, or devices. There are paid programs that can vary in price.

Using a mixture of the two is likely what you will end up doing since not every book will have an audiobook format.

#6

Get Multisensory

Multisensory learning is a great way to teach children who have dyslexia. There are several spelling and reading programs that have been designed for children with dyslexia that are based on multisensory learning.

What exactly is multisensory learning? It is the theory that many people will learn better when they use more than one sense. It doesn't have anything to do with a person's style of learning. Most multisensory programs will use kinesthetic, auditory, tactile, and visual activities.

Multisensory learning has lots of research that supports it. According to the International Dyslexia Association, multisensory teaching is the best way to help children who have dyslexia. Effectively teaching dyslexic children is intensive, cumulative, direct, explicit, and focused on language structure. Multisensory learning uses kinesthetic-tactile, auditory, and visual pathways at the same time to help with learning and memorizing what they read. Links are constantly being made between what we see, what we hear, and what we feel when we are learning to spell and read.

There are several great reading programs that work the best with readers who keep struggling. These are Woodin Math, Lindamood-Bell, Barton, Wilson, and Orton-Gillingham. Many schools who work with dyslexic children use these programs. These programs are a bit expensive, and if you aren't able to purchase them, you could use some of the activities listed later in this chapter.

When you use multisensory teachings doesn't mean you will have your students move when they work, show them videos, or use pictures. The main thing to do is to use at least two or more senses simultaneously. When you have your child say and sound while tracing the letter, you are teaching them multisensory tactics. If you just have the child trace the letter, this isn't multisensory learning.

Since multisensory learning involves using more than two senses while learning, as a parent, you need to give your child a lot of activities that make them use their hands and minds like building a three-dimensional map allows them to see and touch what they are learning. If you use fruits or vegetables to teach your child, fractions can add taste, touch, smell, and sight to something that is hard for anyone to learn.

In normal learning, children normally use about two senses at a time like hearing and sight. Students will see the words when they read and they can hear people when they talk to them. Most dyslexic children will have problems processing auditory and visual information. When you can include more senses, it can make lessons come alive when you can incorporate taste, smell, and touch to your lessons. You will be able to reach your child more and help them retain and learn information. Some of the ideas below are going to take a bit more effort but could bring them help in huge ways.

Quick Facts

☆ Lets you help them learn on their level

☆ Could be used in all subjects from drama, science, math, and reading

☆ Great for anyone but works best for dyslexic children

☆ Can help children find the techniques and learning style that works best for them

☆ Various methods will activate different areas of the brain

☆ Uses kinesthetic, tactile, auditory, and visual elements during learning.

It Isn't Only a Song and Dance

Were you lucky enough to have a teacher who let you dance while learning math, painted during physical education, or sung during science? If you did, you already know a little bit about multisensory learning. This type of teaching doesn't have to be crazy because using your fingers to count is multisensory. It does go beyond the normal approach that completely relies on hearing and vision. This is found when you sit and listen to someone talk to just reading a book. For anyone who is dyslexic, it is a way that needs to be explored more.

Multisensory learning can tap into your tactile, auditory, and visual senses along with kinesthetic, but there are times when tactile and kinesthetic get put together. Teaching approaches that use smell and taste together are extremely rare outside of cooking or wine tasting courses. It would be great to use a reading program that uses food.

You will find a short description of these techniques below.

Kinesthetic

Children who learn by doing and motions will use both their gross and fine motor skills. They are sometimes called tactile learners. It is best to distinguish the two since touch and motions aren't exactly the same. Kinesthesia is what we use when learning how to do physical activities and sports like dancing, golfing, and walking.

The most common kinesthetic method that is used for dyslexic children is having them "air write." This is when a child will say a letter aloud while they write it in the air. This technique dates back to Samuel Orton. You can use this technique in either plasticine or sand. Basically, anything that can connect the body's movements to learning is kinesthetic. This can be anything from clapping out a rhythm or jumping rope to help teach long division.

Tactile

Tactile learning is anything that involves touch. Most of the time this will overlap with kinesthetic learning. Tactile techniques engage fine motor skills.

Some specific techniques might include using finger paints, textures, raised line paper, sand, poker chips, dominoes, coins, and letter tiles. Small puzzles like a Rubik's cube use tactile learning. Materials like plasticine or clay are great learning media for tactile learning.

Auditory

Ben Foss is a champion and dyslexic author. He loves finding the difference between ear and eye reading. This is another great idea to help your dyslexic child. You can absolutely read with your ears when you use text to speech and audiobooks. With some practice, you could learn to listen at extremely high speeds.

Learning to read doesn't depend on reading words in books. This point doesn't get emphasized enough with dyslexic children. I'll say it again: Learning to read doesn't depend on just reading words in books.

Some examples of auditory learning include dialogue, clapping, lyrics, audio tones, rhymes, singing, and music; basically, anything that involves using your ears.

Visual

Using vision when teaching is anything from visual arts to reading the text in books. Video, posters, painting, or any creative visual design can be used to teach.

Brainstorming sessions that result in a visual map that links ideas could be extremely effective for a written research poster or paper.

Visual aids could help along with tactile or auditory learning, like showing musical notes on paper or with pictures about how to knit or sew.

How To Create a Multisensory House

It doesn't matter if you are homeschooling your child or are working closely with your child's teacher. To make sure your child succeeds in life, you have to both be on the same page. You can use the following to help your child learn whether they are just beginning to learn or need some help in the classroom.

☆ Create Games

You could easily create a game of trivial pursuit to help your child review their social studies or science homework. When you make reviewing exciting and fun, it can help your child remember their lessons.

☆ Use Various Kinds of Media

You can help your child with their homework by having manipulatives or pictures that you can let your child hold, see, and touch the information. Try to make every lesson as interactive and unique as possible will keep your child interested and can help them retain all the information.

☆ Encourage Discussions

If your child is having a hard time learning, encourage them to talk to you about what parts they are having problems with. This allows your child a chance to talk about things that might be bothering them. Your child might be reluctant to talk to their teacher about something that they are having problems learning, but when you allow them to talk to you, this helps them get it off their mind and out of their system. They see that you are really interested in helping them learn.

☆ Using Colored Paper

Rather than just using white paper, have colored paper handy to make doing homework fun. Use yellow paper on Wednesdays, green paper on Fridays, and pink on Monday. This breaks up the monotony and keeps their attention.

☆ Make Stories Come Alive

Help your child create a puppet show or skit to help them act out what they are reading. If you have more than one child, have them work together to create a play and allow them to perform it after dinner for the family.

☆ Begin With an Object or Picture

There might be times when your child is asked to write a story, then illustrate it, draw a picture to show their math problems, or write a book report and find photos that go with it. Rather than doing that, begin with the object or picture. Ask your child to find a picture in a magazine and then write a story about what they see is happening in the picture. You could also give them a piece of fruit and ask them to write some descriptive words about the fruit.

☆ Using Scents to Show Feelings

Many people have often wondered if smells can affect a person's work performance or mood. People who are in a room that smells good have used efficient work strategies, set better goals, and have a higher self-efficacy. You can use aromatherapy in your house to help your child. Here are some normal beliefs about scents:

- Cinnamon can help with focus

- Pine, peppermint, and citrus can help with alertness

- Vanilla and lavender helps with relaxing

You might find your child will react differently to specific scents, so you might have to experiment with some fragrances to find what works best for your child.

☆ Using Music

You can set grammar rules, spelling words, or math facts to music, just like you taught them the alphabet by singing the alphabet song to them when they were young. You can play soothing music during homework or if they are working quietly by themselves.

☆ Different Colors for Different Parts of Their Room

You can set their room or homework area up to help promote creativity and motivate them. Green colors can help with feeling well and concentration. This would be good to have near a computer or reading areas.

☆ Writing Down Assignments

You and your child's teacher could use various colors for every subject and when making notes in books. You could use green for math, yellow for history, or red for spelling. Add a plus sign beside anything that they need an extra book or other materials for. The various colors let your student know just by looking what subjects they have homework in and what they need to take home.

Things You Can Do

If you aren't sure ways to apply multisensory activities or if you are looking for some inspirations, you can do some of the following:

☆ Multisensory Activities for Math

- Whole body facts
- Games
- Music

- Drawing
- Visual representations
- Manipulatives that show operations and equations

☆ Multisensory Activities for Reading

- Games
- Use nonsense words
- Adding movements for sounds of letters
- Show them what diacritical marks are for
- Make words with magnetic letters, cards, and tiles
- Sandpaper writing
- Air writing
- Tap out sounds
- Letters that are colored coded
- Phonogram cards to help with sound association

☆ Multisensory Activities for Spelling

- Whole body spelling activities

- Games
- Playdough
- Show how to use diacritical marks
- Make picture associations
- Say the sound while writing
- Air writing
- Tap out sounds
- Tap out letters

Final Thoughts

Multisensory learning gives your child more ways they can learn new information, ways to recall it later, and ways to remember it. Children who are dyslexic normally have problems absorbing new things, especially if it involves memorizing steps or sequences. These multisensory techniques can help break these barriers down to help make abstract learning more concrete, turning sequences or lists into sounds, sights, and movements.

The best part of multisensory learning is it works well and is fun for every child. It needs to be a part of everyone's toolbox.

Create Homework Time

Dyslexic children spend a large amount of energy every day during school. Their brains work a lot harder to process spelling, writing, and reading than a child who doesn't have dyslexia. By the end of their school day, they are completely exhausted. Most of these children will have homework they need to do, and some might even need to be tutored. Dyslexic children want to be just like everybody else and do extracurricular activities, music, or sports. How can we, as parents or caregivers, help our child balance all of this?

When my daughter was nine, she was diagnosed with a mild form of dyslexia. It caused big problems when it was time to do homework. I knew it was hard for her to read, but she got extremely upset if we helped her repeat a word. It became such a problem that I was ready to stop trying to help her keep up and just allow her to fail. I turned to the internet to see if I could find some ideas on what I could do to help. Here is what I found:

Dyslexic children who grew up to be successful adults will tell you they became successful either because they had the drive or someone was there who encouraged them. They might tell you that they had a mentor or coach who helped them stay on track even when things were rough. Teenagers who have dyslexia will normally talk about an adult who handled their outbursts or tantrums and got them back to their work.

They might tell you that the outbursts were a way of expressing their frustrations. It might have been a way to get out of reading, but at times the arguments and outbursts were from their feelings of embarrassment or shame. They knew they couldn't read as well as their classmates and they didn't want to let their parents down. If you are tired of the constant battles, maybe you could find someone who can be the "pusher." This lets children and parents do things together that can focus on the child's positive traits, while others keep pressuring them to do their reading. This person could be a friend, grandparent, or a teacher who is willing to work with your child after hours. It might be easier to find a tutor that you can pay. Look at college or high school students who are looking to become a teacher.

The main thing I had to realize was I had to let my child know that I believed in her, and I knew she could do better with time if she has the right type of help. I realized that I was not the right person to do this at that time. Somebody had to help my daughter realize that she was having problems reading due to her dyslexia and not because she was dumb. Her teachers began working with her more closely and were able to give this message to her. Her teachers also began holding her accountable for doing her homework. Once she realized that she would be missing recess or staying after school to do her homework, this helped her stay on task. Her teachers started giving her a more reasonable type and amount of homework.

Giving in or giving up wasn't the answer if I wanted my daughter to be a successful adult who has dyslexia. I found some articles and videos that showed her children of different ages talking about their dyslexia and how it made them feel. It helped her realize that she wasn't alone in this ordeal, and there is hope for children who have problems reading.

Homework Strategies

As you can see from above, homework can be an upsetting and frustrating experience for parents and children who have dyslexia daily. Try the following tips to make the experience better.

☆ Monitoring and Checking Their Work

You can help your child learn to check their skills, monitor themselves, and edit their work so they can check their own work as they age. A simple checking process such as COPS could be helpful when proofreading their work.

C stands for Capitals

O stands for Overall appearance

P stands for Punctuation

S stands for Spelling

You can show your child how to use a computer when they get older. Teach them to use a spell checker and help them learn how to type. Above all else, give them praise when they finish a homework task. Be as specific as you can about what they did well.

☆ Get Started

Try to chunk their homework into sections that you know they can manage and give them breaks in between each task. Children who have dyslexia get discouraged when they are faced with a lot of work. Give your child encouragement to produce their best work instead of rushing through.

Go over the requirements of their homework to make sure they know what they need to do. Read any instructions out loud if you know it is hard for them to understand them. If you have to, give them an example.

Help them create ideas for projects and tasks before they begin working on them. If you have to, change up the vocabulary that they might need. You could help them create a writing plan. When you know it is appropriate and needed, write for your child so they can put their ideas on paper.

Help them present their work by using their strengths such as pictures if they like and are good at art.

☆ Homework Routine

You need to create a daily routine for homework. This can be visual or written but it needs to be put in a place that your child can see it well. It needs to have an agreed plan about what happens after they come home from school. Have some flexibility about after-school activities. Figure out what the best time would be for your child to do their homework. Remember that they are going to be extremely tired after school since they have to work harder than the other children, so they might need a break before they begin their homework.

Reading each day is very important because a lot of practice is needed for dyslexic children to master reading. When your child gets frustrated, read out loud to them. This will help them enjoy and understand what they are reading and they are still learning. Your child could read along with audiobooks, too.

☆ Make Sure Homework is Reasonable

You need to remember that the main reason for homework is to practice things that your child is familiar with. If their homework is too hard, you need to talk about this with their teacher. Never allow your child to get so frustrated since homework tasks take too long or are beyond their skill level. Giving them extra time or less work will sometimes help.

☆ Take a Break or Do Homework

This has to be up to you and your child. If they work better after they have a snack, then give them a snack or better yet, let them eat a snack while they start their homework. Some children need a break after they have spent all day at school. Other children just want to get it over with. If homework is taking too long, write a note to their teacher to let them know how long it is taking them to finish their homework. This way, if they don't finish it, they can see that the child spent a certain amount of time on it. My best friend realized that her child did better if she gave him time to unwind after school. They would go on a 15 minute walk, they had a snack and rested for 30 minutes when they got home, then they tackled the homework. They knew that homework had to be done before sports practice began. That brings me to my next point.

☆ Homework Versus Sports

This one is hard, but sometimes it is important to do your best to fit both of them in. Since my daughter started high school, she doesn't have as much time for karate as she did. I give her a push to continue it. She does feel better after she gets some physical activity. We find the time for her tutoring since just having a person sitting next to you can motivate you. My friend's children were always up before the sun so she decided to tutor her children before school since they were too busy with sports after school. Be sure you don't allow homework to take over their extra-curricular activities. You need to let your child engage in things that they like to do and are good at. Tutoring can be scheduled around other activities.

☆ Writing for Them or Reading to Them

When my daughter was still in elementary, I allowed her to turn her work in without it being edited. As she got older, she wanted to turn in work that had been corrected and finished. We decided to submit her work in two batches. One was her own work without being edited and the other was what she got help with. Elementary school reading was done by me out loud or through audiobooks.

My daughter's friend ear reads for 30 minutes rather than eye reading for 20. His parents try not to jump in and help too much. They do help read any questions, clear up directions, and write down their answers if he needed them to but their work needs to be their work. They submit their homework with some notes about how long it took them and what they helped him with.

Never greet them with: "What is your homework?" Try to have a routine and structure.

How to Create a Homework Station

As stated above, homework can be the source of too much drama at home from: "Is your homework done?" "Have you seen my backpack?" to "Where is my notebook?"

Rather than feeding the drama, why not make your home a place of calm in the middle of all the chaos. Set your child up for success by making a homework station.

Teaching a child how to get organized and keeping themselves organized is a very important skill. Tasks like project preparation, tidying up their workspace, and time management won't just help them do their school work, but with their life choices and all the challenges it can bring as they grow and learn.

As parents, we need to use these tips to make a homework station for elementary school children. These could also be applied to anyone who wants to update their existing homework station for a child of any age.

Your children are going to love their homework space that they might be excited enough to just do their homework.

What Is a Homework Station?

This is a designated, inviting workspace where a child can finish their homework and study.

A good area will give the child an uncluttered surface where they can draw and write, all the supplies that they are going to need to complete their work, and a comfortable space for them to read.

Giving a child a homework station is important since it will give them a space that they know is to be used for them to learn. These spaces don't have to be fancy, expensive, or huge. They just need to be easily accessible and have everything a child might need.

Find The Space

You are going to need to find a space or room that will work for your child. It all depends on how much help they need and their age; this could be in the family room or kitchen or a desk in their own room.

A homework station doesn't have to be at a table or desk. A comfortable place in the corner with pillows and a lap desk would work as long as there isn't anything that is going to distract your child from their tasks at hand.

The main guideline for the homework station is the space needs to be free from interruptions, distractions, and noise. An older child needs to sit at a table rather than the floor as this helps them establish good habits and can help them work on their handwriting. They will also have the room to spread out their stuff.

The space needs to be supportive and comfortable. You don't want to have a chair that is your child's excuse for not doing their homework at the space you created.

Make sure you have a trash bin close to their work station so they won't throw their papers on the floor but will put them in the trash. It will also encourage them to throw the garbage out of their backpacks regularly.

What Your Child Needs

Before you create a space that YOU love, ask your child what they need. Creating a space where your child can function is extremely important. Think about how productive you are when your work area has everything you want and need to use. You won't be wasting time looking for supplies, and your workday goes a lot better.

Your child could be more efficient if their homework station was arranged just like your workspace. Just ask them what they need to be able to do their homework.

You might be surprised to hear that it is simple things like fidget tools, pencil sharpeners, or a timer. It this is what it takes to make the homework station perfect for them, you will be able to fulfill their request easily.

Get Rid of Clutter

Clutter can create chaos. It causes a feeling that everything has to be rushed, and nothing will ever get done completely. If your child wants to use the desk in their room, make sure that nothing else is on the desk.

If they start putting other things in the desk like craft projects, LEGOs, books, etc. all they are doing is putting distractions close by that will pull them away from their homework.

☆ Wall Organization

You can hang up a pin, magnetic, or corkboard for your child to put a calendar, reminders, or papers on. This space needs to be within reach of their desk so that they can remove or add important items regularly. It can give them a chance to personalize and decorate their space. Hopefully, this will inspire them to use it.

☆ Desk Organization

Your child needs to have supplies within their reach to keep them productive. They shouldn't need to take 12 trips around the house trying to find what they need to finish their homework or projects.

If there is room on their desk, think about keeping supplies organized in a neat little container.

Any type of organizer can be moved easily since there might be times when your child isn't going to be home when they do their homework. Find an organizer that holds all the supplies they are going to need, so they don't have any excuse not to do their homework.

Make putting away their supplies easy by putting labels on all the supply caddies and containers. This teaches them how to keep their space clean, and maybe they will stop asking you where they should put things.

As your child ages, homework might require them to use a computer or other technology. This means there is going to be chaos with charging and cords. Try to keep the space tidy from the cords by using products to keep the cables handy and neat when it is time to charge.

☆ Managing Their Subjects

You can help keep your child's subjects organized by using file folders of various colors so they can keep notes organized in their book bag and their desk. A file folder organizer can help them keep their homework within reach. If there isn't enough room on their desk, try one that hangs on the wall.

☆ In and Out Bins

There is a lot of paperwork that needs to get to your hands safely. Think about getting some in and out bins that your child can put any paper that might need to be seen or signed by you. You can check them every night and then put any that should go back to the school in the out bin so your child can grab them the next morning. With some practice, this is a great method that can be utilized through high school.

☆ Calendar

It is very important that a child learns ways to manage their own calendar. It doesn't matter if it is a desktop planner or a large calendar that you hang on the wall and use dry erase markers on. This is a good way for them to see with assignments and tests they have coming up so that they can manage their time wisely.

Create a Routine

It might be tempting to allow your child to do their homework in a different room every day. This completely defeats the purpose of instilling discipline and study skills. If your child asks if they can do their homework some other place, you can tell them how important it is to keep a constant homework routine.

After you get their homework space organized, help them create a routine about when to do their homework. It might be when they get home from school. Maybe they work better after they've had a snack, or maybe after dinner. Whatever works for them, help them stick to this routine by setting a timer or giving them some gentle guidance. Hopefully, since they have their new homework station, they will feel excited and be ready to work.

Creating Good Habits

You need to make sure you give your child the tools that they need to manage their time by having a timer or clock at their homework station. You can set a time limit for every subject as this helps them remain on track and is a life skill that will go with them throughout their life.

There is a product called the Time Timer. It shows your child the amount of time they have left for a task. It's easy for them to set, and they won't need to know to tell time to understand that their time is going away.

Once they finish their homework, think about helping them create a routine that will help them make their morning a little less hectic. It might be as simple as doing a backpack check the night before to make sure all their papers and books are ready for the next day. You could have them put their backpack in a special place close to the front door, so they don't have to hunt for it the next morning.

Homework Supplies

The supplies that a child will need at their homework station are going to vary for each child and their ages. Your elementary school child might need rulers, watercolors, markers, crayons, colored pencils, scissors, glue, pencils, drawing paper, and wide-ruled paper.

Middle and high school children may need a graphing calculator, scientific, highlighters, index cards, college-ruled paper, graph paper, pens, and pencils.

It doesn't matter what their age, every child would benefit from some floor pillows, a lap desk, a computer, a desk, a desk lamp, and a supply caddy.

Strategies to Help Homework Go Smoother

There are two main strategies that parents can use to reduce homework problems. The first would be to establish a good routine as stated above that includes where and when homework needs to be done and then set daily schedules for doing homework. The next one is to create an incentive or rewards program to give to the child when they do their homework or get "good grades."

Incentive and Reward Program

Most children who aren't motivated by simply doing homework get motivated by the grades that they hope to get as the result of doing good schoolwork. Therefore, their grades are their incentive and this is what motivates them to do their homework in a timely manner and with care. For dyslexic children who don't get motivated by grades, you are going to have to look for other ways to help them get through their homework. Incentive and reward programs can fall into two different categories: elaborate and simple.

☆ Elaborate

This involves more work and planning on your part as a parent, but there are sometimes when you might have to address specific homework problems. Elaborate incentive rewards might include ways to earn points that they can use to "buy" rewards or privileges. You could also have a separate system that gives better rewards for doing hard or complicated homework. These systems will work best if the child and parent can work together to create them. Allowing the child to have some input will give them a sense of ownership and control. The system will succeed better if they have some input. Children are normally realistic when setting goals and figuring out rewards and penalties when they get a say so in making the decisions.

☆ Simple

The simplest reward is just reminding your child about a fun activity that you told them they could do once their homework is finished. This could be allowing them to watch their favorite television show, time to play a video game, texting or talking on the phone, or playing a special game with their friends. The program of withholding anything fun until homework is done is referred to as "Grandma's Law" because grandmothers have a tendency to use if very effectively like: "Take out the trash first and then you get to have a cookie." When a child has something to look forward to, it can be a great incentive to get homework done. Once a parent reminds their child of this when they sit down to do their homework, they might be able to spark the fire that makes the child stick to the task until it is finished.

☆ Adding in Choices

This is a great strategy for parents to implement with children who have a hard time doing their homework. Choice could be incorporated into the order that the child agrees to do their homework and then the schedule they have to follow in order to do the work. Adding in choices doesn't just help motivate a child, but it could reduce power struggles.

☆ Adding in Breaks

These are great for children who can't make it through to the end without getting some small reward. When you are creating your child's homework schedule, it might be helpful for the child to be able to know when they can take a break. One child might like to take a break at a certain time while others take a break once they finish a subject. If you use this kind of approach, you need to talk to your child about how long of a break they can take and what they will do during their break like playing one level of a game, call a friend, or get a snack.

Creating the Incentive Program

☆ Figuring Out the Bad Behavior

The child and parent need to figure out which behaviors are causing the problems during homework. For some, it is the child putting off doing their homework until the last minute. For others, it is forgetting books or materials or forgetting to write down what needs to be done. While others will rush through their homework and do it wrong. Other children take hours to finish what should have only taken then a couple of minutes. You have to be extremely specific when you describe their problem behaviors. This has to be described as behaviors that can be heard or seen like: rushes through homework, complains about homework, and makes a lot of mistakes.

☆ Set Goals

Normally the goal is going to relate to the problem behavior. For example, if they constantly forget to write down their assignments, the goal could be: "Judy will write down her assignments in her assignment book for each class."

☆ Penalties and Rewards

Homework incentives work best when a child has a menu of rewards to choose from because there isn't one reward that will attract them for too long. A point system where points can be earned for the behavior goal gets traded in for the reward they want to earn. The larger the reward, the more points they will have to earn. The menu has to include both smaller and larger rewards. It might be necessary to create penalties for the system. This is normally losing certain privileges like losing their television or game time.

When you have your reward system done, and you see that your child is getting more penalties than rewards, then you need to revise your program so that the child can become more successful. When this kind of failure happens, we consider it a design failure instead of the childs failure. It could be a good idea if you are having a hard time figuring out a system that works for your child, to talk with a school counselor or specialist for help.

#8

Color Code

We all spend around 21,000 hours in school. That does not include after school classes or homework. That is quite a bit of hours and a bunch more work. It is hard enough to get through all of this for a regular student, now imagine how it feels if you suffer from a learning disability, like dyslexia, to fight on top of all of that.

If you breakdown the skill of reading, it's easy to see that it is a very complicated skill, and reading specialists understand that hundreds of skills are involved in the process. This makes it very taxing and there are some children who like to use colored overlays to help clear the print and lower their visual stress.

But luckily, we have many different ways to help children overcome the stress of dyslexia and improve their learning abilities, and one such way is through color coding. There have been studies done on the power of color and dyslexia. The theory behind this is simple. You want to help the brain create a connection between the chosen color and the shape of the letter. This will help to speed up the learning process, improve the reading rate, reading accuracy, and comprehension.

Color coding is especially helpful for those between the ages of five and ten, who tend to have the hardest time learning to read. The method gives them a nearly instantaneous deliverance. They will nearly automatically find reading easier, which will lead to more motivation and an improved self-image.

Kobi successfully adopted The Color Coding system, which is a mobile app that helps teach children how to read. It was carefully created for children who have reading difficulties, like dyslexia, and has shown promising results. During their test, 100 education professionals worked with over 500 kids who battled dyslexia, and they found around 93.63% of them showed significant improvement in their reading comprehension, reading accuracy, and reading rate after reading with Kobi.

Kobi works by changing the color of letters that the child is struggling with to help them recognize the letter. It also has the ability for you to take a picture of text and have it converted to Kobi, so a child can use the software to read a school assignment. It also comes with text-to-speech. That way if your child finds a word they don't know how to pronounce, Kobi can help them. But this is only one form of color coding that can help children with dyslexia.

Colored Overlays

Another form of color coding includes the use of color overlays. This is placed over a block of text to help the child see and read the text better.

According to Professor Arnold Wilkins and his colleagues, the use of colored overlays helps to "reduce the symptoms of visual stress and increase reading fluency in about 20% of school children. In 5% of children, the increase in speed with overlays is greater than 25%."

They have a website where they explain colored overlays and you can get an overlay testing kit to find out which color of overlay is going to help your child the most. They are comprised of several sheets of different color acetate, which can be placed over the text. In their testing procedure, pairs of colors successively compared and the child is asked to judge which one of the colors makes the text easier to read. This is called the Wilkins Rate of Reading Test, and can then be used to help measure how much improvement the chosen color brought about.

Reading involves a number of skills, which include teaming and focusing, eye tracking, cognitive skills, decoding words, sounds that symbols represent, symbol recognition, perception, along with hundreds of other things. Therefore, reading is a lot more complicated than many of us think. When a child is struggling with dyslexia, reading ends up become a lot more complicated because the letters end up looking like they move around, change color, and might appear wave-life.

Dr. Stephen Guffanti, an expert on howtolearn.com, went throughout medical school, rarely reading his text, and not even realizing that he had dyslexia. One day, he and his wife were reading the paper together. He asked her, "What do you do when the words move around because you are reading so much faster than I read?"

He then realized that using colored overlays were able to help steady the words on the page, and he started to recommend them to his patients. He found that for some people who were diagnosed with dyslexia, it ended up being more a visual perceptual problem that could be fixed through vision therapy and colored overlays.

There are many different benefits to using colored overlays. They definitely make a lot of people more comfortable and able to read for longer periods of time. Colored overlays help to relax the eyes, and even your shoulders and neck as you read. Colored overlays will definitely help to improve the comprehension of the text because they are actually able to read what is written.

Color Coded Schedules

We've talked about the importance of having a routine set for your child. Along those lines, you should think about color coding their schedule. Now, the act of coloring coding your calendar is actually something that can help everybody because it helps to keep things balanced and keep you mindful of what's going on. It will also be useful in finding areas where there tends to be a loss of focus.

We all want to experience different types of activities. The brain requires and craves different types of activities physiologically. When we end up engaging in too little or too much of a certain task, we habituate. To habituate means that you end up getting used to what you are thinking or doing and you become immune to the emotions that it creates. When you maintain a healthy variety of tasks, chores, experiences, and people, it will keep your brain engaged.

It's important that you keep your child's schedule on one calendar so that they can see the balance between work and play. This plays into the whole work/life balance that we adults are supposed to have figured out.

Now, before you begin to randomly assign colors to tasks or events on your child's calendar, you have to realize that different colors will represent different things to their brains. Understanding that colors mean different things to different people is not really groundbreaking. The color concept has been used for years in marketing and advertising.

The first thing we need to do is go over what colors mean. Yellow represents optimism, clarity, and warmth. This is the reason why yellow is used by brands like Denny's, National Geographic, Best Buy, IKEA, and McDonald's. The other colors are:

- ☆ Green – health, peaceful, growth

- ☆ Blue – strong, trustworthy, dependable, and can be used for brainstorming, networking, and presenting

- ☆ Purple – imaginative, creative, wise

- ☆ Red – youthful, exciting, bold, it also represents power and energy, and can be used for urgent tasks

- ☆ Orange – confident, friendly, cheerful, wealth, luxury, and can represent new or long-term projects that are focused upon the future

- ☆ Yellow – optimism, clarity, warmth, and can be used for production tasks or to share new ideas

- ☆ Pink – love, compassion, and can be used for special occasions and personal labels

☆ Black – power, and prestige

☆ White – perfection, success, purity

With that in mind, you can begin to color code calendars so that they make sense.

- Grey represents school

Grey represents balance, so grey should be used to represent the time your child is in school. Using a bland color for school helps to maintain a balance that is needed in order to make school successful.

- Red represents homework

Research from the University of British Columbia found that red "is the most effective at enhancing our attention to detail." Red is best to use for tasks that will need your undivided attention.

- Purple should be used for creative tasks

Since purple is representative of wisdom, creativity, and imagination, it is the best color to use when you are blocking out time for creative tasks.

- Blue should be used for less-important tasks

Blue often triggers feelings of relaxation in the brain. Since it is a relaxation color, it makes it a great color when you schedule breaks throughout your child's day. Another color you could choose for relaxing tasks is pink because it is calming.

- Green represents meal times

Green is connected to tranquility and health; as such, you should use this to mark off their meal times during the day.

- Use white for prep

White represents simplicity and happiness, so that means you can use it for those critical prep sessions that your child may have during the day. This could be times before they have a test or presentation at school so that you can spend extra time with them to get ready.

You can also use this color coding strategies with the homework, studying, and presentations your child has to do. Each week, get with your child and write out a to-do list for the things they are going to be faced with during the week. A regular running task is going to be daily homework. Other things that might change could be if they have a book report that they have a couple of weeks to do, a school presentation, practice work they do with you, or studying for tests.

After you have written these things down, the two of your designate a certain color to each task. For example, you may use red for tasks that have to be done right away, like homework, and you can use green for tasks that aren't as important.

You can also use colors in various other areas of your child's life, like organizing the different subjects in school. Adding color will help both you and your child to save time in doing and retrieving information. Likewise, if they have multiple projects, they are working on for school, assigning a different color to each of them will help to make fast work of the tasks. The main reason for color coding is to allow somebody to be able to visually and quickly identify different categories, thus giving the brain a bit of a break.

Adding some color to your child's life will not only improve their function in school and studies, but it will help to lower their stress. They will feel better when they are able to easily locate what they are supposed to be doing and spend their time on the task instead of trying to figure out what is next.

#9

Reading Assisters

When we are reading any sort of content, our eyes have to make small stops after a few words in a sentence. However, those who struggle to read tend to make several more stops, which reduces their reading speed and slows or inhibits their comprehension. Contrasting background colors and font can make it harder for them to focus and track smooth line transitions. There are reading tools and tricks that can help eliminate or reduce these reading issues for dyslexics.

The eyes work in a very specific way. When an object moves across your vision field, your eyes move to maintain fixation. Visual tracking happens when a person's eyes move along a single in an accurate and smooth manner. When you move your eyes, there are two main types of eye movements that you use to gather information: visual pursuits and saccadic eye movements.

Visual pursuits, which is tracking, is able to occur when you move only your eyes or when you move your head and eyes together. Your visual tracking will depend on visual attention as well as fatigue

Saccadic movement, often known as saccades, is the ability of your eyes to move from point A to B rapidly without them deviating from their path.

Children and adults who suffer from reading troubles need strategies and tools to help improve their reading success. In can be hard for them to get focused on reading a full sentence and then start to process the information correctly. A lot of education methods will fail to meet the three basic needs for effective support for struggling readers:

1. Help the reader to focus more easily on lines of text or part of the page

2. Allow the reader to concentrate on single words or lines when they need to

3. Encourage eye movement from left to right and from one line to the next

We're going to look at a few different tools that will accomplish these three things to ensure your child gets the help they need.

Reading Strips

Reading strips are practical tools to help assist children to better concentrate, visualize, and retain the information that they are reading. They tend to be a ruler sized strip with a transparent shaded cutout window that they will put over the text that they are reading.

The reading strips will help them to control the movement of their eyes while reading, and it eliminates problems like skilling words and sentences, reading the same sentence multiple times, losing concentration, swapping out letters, and reading too close to the paper.

To use the reading strip, they will place the strip onto the page, making sure that they can see the words that need to be read through the cutout window. They move the strip across and down the page as they are reading to help maintain concentration and to track the upcoming information. The colored, transparent portion helps to filter out distractions without blocking the entire context.

Reading strips are able to be used with all types of reading material. Most are made to fit nearly all commonly used font sizes. You can also find some that are made for on-screen reading.

Line Tracker

These reading trackers are fun ways to help your child read. They work similar to the reading strips mentioned above, but they don't have the colored strip. These are silly tracking tools that your child can make their selves, which may be a motivation in and of itself. To make these trackers, you are going to need:

☆ Scissors

☆ Crafting tape

☆ Adhesive googly eyes

☆ Colored popsicles sticks – medium size

First, let them pick out a popsicle stick in a color that they like to make their tracker. Next, let them decorate the stick with some of the crafting tape, leaving a space at the top for the googly eye. Once they are done decorating, have them press a googly eye onto the tracker. The eye end is the end that they use to track their reading.

Not only will these decorated sticks make fun reading trackers for your kids, but they can also double a bookmark. All they need to do to use the tracker is to move it under the line of text that they are reading to help them keep their place.

Visual Tracker

This tracking tool will require coordinated movements of both hands and eyes. The integrated movements of both arms and crossing the midline are important for directionality and laterality. These are areas that are needed in reading and writing numbers and letters without reversals. This is another tracking tool you can make yourself. You will need:

☆ Clay

☆ Wooden skewer

☆ Scissors

☆ Drinking straw

First, cut off a quarter inch section from the straw and then slip it over the skewer. Then roll up a ball of clay a press it onto the end of the skewer, repeat on the other side. That's it.

This tracking tool has multiple uses. First, you can use it to help your child train their eyes for smoother tracking. In order to practice smooth visual pursuit, tilt the skewer from side to side, and have your child watch the straw as it moves. You can let them use the tracking tool themselves and ask them to follow the straw.

You can also use this tool as a math practice. Place the tracking tool along a number line. Tilt it from side to side, and when it stops at a number, ask them what the number is. You can also expand this by asking them to subtract or add the various numbers that the straw stops at.

You can also align the tracking tool under a number line and then use the straw as a placeholder as your child counts the subtraction and addition problems along the line. You can also place it under a line of text. The straw can be moved along the length of the skewer as your child reads out the words in the sentences.

Another way to use the tracker is to hold it up horizontally and ask your child to look quickly from one clay ball to the other. This is where you may want to use different colored clay balls for each end so that they can say out the color name when their eyes focus on it. They can do the same thing as you hold the skewer vertically. Lastly, hold it in a diagonal position and have them look from one ball to the other.

Sight Words

Sight words are commonly heard when it comes to reading and has several meanings. For the most part, it refers to a set of about 100 words that show up frequently in texts. Besides the fact that they show up frequently, a lot of them are unable to be "sounded out." This is why children are expected to learn them all by sight. Unfortunately, this will often mean minimal teaching. Often times, little is done other than showing them the word and telling the child what it says. For a lot of children, this isn't enough. As a reference, the following are the most common sight words that children have to learn.

A. After, about, all, and, at, as, are, at, an, a

B. Been, but, by, be

C. Called, could, can

D. Do, down, did

E. Each

F. For, find, first, from

H. Him, have, her, has, how, had, his, he

I. Its, it, is, into, if, I, in

J. Just

K. Know

L. Little, long, like

M. Most, many, more, make, may, made, my

N. Now, no, not

O. On, only, over, other, out, of, one, or

P. People

S. See, so, some, she, said

T. Their, that, than, time, two, these, then, them, there, this, they, to, the

U. Use, up

V. Very

W. Way, who, water, where, words, would, will, which, we, when, were, what, with, was

X. Your, you

Children with dyslexia will often have a hard time learning sight words. It gets even trickier due to the face that many of the words don't follow standard rules for spelling, which makes them unable to be decoded. Some of the words appear so frequently that children will have to be able to recognize the word quickly in order to be fluent readers. The following tips will help you to teach your child how to learn these sight words.

1. Focus On The Detail

Those who have reading difficulties might have to have help in noticing the details in the words they learn, especially if it is one that is hard to spell. For example, the word "through." Start by showing them the word and saying it aloud. Then ask them to say the letters. Then ask them to pick out the vowels they see. Then ask which letters make up the first, middle, and end of the word. This teaches them how to analyze the word and take in its details

2. Create Memory Tricks

There are times when children can come up with a trick to help them memorize words that cause them trouble. These are what is known as mnemonics. They can create a rhyme using the word they need to remember, or something that they are able to associate with the word. They may also want to make up a phrase to help them spell it. Let's pretend that they are having a hard time remembering them. You could provide them with the mnemonic, "**Th**ey **E**at **Y**ams."

3. Get Creative

Some children find it easier to remember sight words if they are able to connect it with an image. Here is a way in which you can do that. Write out a practice word on two sides of a flashcard. On one of the sides, you, or your child, should draw a picture into the word, such as drawing eyes inside of the o's in the word look. Introduce those practice words using those illustrations. Once your child is able to the word easily and quickly, start showing them the printed side only.

4. Take a Mental Photo

Ask your child to take a look at the written word, and then ask them to "take a picture of it" and then hold that picture in their mind. Then remove the card. Ask them what letters they are able to still see in their mind. What are the first, second, and last letters, or vowels? Practicing this visualization can help children remember, read, and spell the words they learn

5. Use a Pencil

After they have got the hang of reading and then air-writing these words, you should have them write it out on paper. Start by having them copy the words off of a flashcard or word list. Then they can try to write them without looking. You may also want to have them write the word a few times on a chalkboard as they say the letters and the word. Or you can ask them to write it out on paper a few times every day. You want them to practice the word until they can consistently spell the word without having to look at it.

6. Learn About Its History

There is normally a reason why a word that can't be sounded out is spelled. There is a rule in the English language that does not allow words to end in a v. This is the reason why we place a silent e on the end of words like have and give. Take the word knife. It originated from knife, an Old Norse word, and they would pronounce the k. Checking out the history of the word can help teach children why it's spelled oddly. It is also helpful for them to learn the meaning of the word. And improving their word knowledge helps them to recognize these words faster.

7. Create a Word Wall

Think about creating a space within your home where you are able to display the words that they have learned and mastered. One option is to use butcher paper, and then you can let them decorate it and once they are done, hang it up in a place where they are able to see it. This gives them something to refer back to for spelling practice and assignments. The words can be written directly on the butcher paper or you can tape the flashcards up on it. This is a great way for you to show your child how much they have learned, which is going to help to boost their self-esteem

8. Search for Words

Ask your child to go through books you have at home and pick out the words that they have been practicing in class. This is going to increase their awareness of how often as certain word gets used. This will also help them with being on the lookout for the word whenever they are reading. Once they have picked out those words, the two of you can read that book. You also need to make sure that you provide them with positive feedback whenever they are correct in reading the target work.

9. Keep Things Manageable

You should start by introducing a single word every one to two days until they have a list of about ten words for them to work on. Add in a new word once your child masters one. This will help to keep their goals more manageable. This will also improve the likelihood that they are going to improve and feel better about their sight word learning. This will help to give them the motivation they need to continue practicing.

Online Help for Dyslexia

While there are many different trackers out there that can help your child read, dyslexic children can also benefit greatly from technology. There are various types of tools and apps available that can help a dyslexic child write, read, and more. There are 11 apps and tools that we will go over that will ensure your child is able to keep up with a 21st century classroom.

1. MindMeister

Traditional note-taking is often difficult for dyslexic children. This is an app that will allow users to create mind maps or graphic organizers to write down their thought easily and quickly.

2. OCR Instantly Pro

Text-to-speech apps are a great tool for online content, but what are they supposed to do about worksheets or books? OCR Instantly Pro gives them the chance to snap a picture of any page and then convert it to text, which will then be read aloud by several different text-to-speech apps.

3. What Is Dyslexia?

This apps is not necessarily just for those who have dyslexia, but it is an amazing tool. It also has a quiz that can help you figure out if your child is dyslexic or is going to need further screening. It also contains information for parents, teachers, and other students so that they can better understand dyslexia.

4. Reading Intro by Oz Phonics

This is another great app for a young reader with dyslexia. Reading Intro by Oz Phonics helps children to learn how to recognize letter sounds.

The tasks of this are simple and fun enough for a child to play all on their own.

5. OpenWeb

OpenWeb is a web browser that is able to convert text into a font that is easy for a dyslexic reader to understand, which allows dyslexic children to read with less difficulty. This is very useful for times when a text-to-speech approach is disruptive or unnecessary.

6. vBooks PDF Voice Reader

There are a lot of text-to-speech apps that are unable to convert PDF documents into speech. This software is able to do just that, and it is also able to change the font to that has been designed for the dyslexic reader.

7. Ginger Page

Dyslexic children will normally have a hard time with spellings. Software that has spellcheck or autocorrect is sometimes unable to figure out what a dyslexic child is trying to write. Ginger Page is an even more sophisticated word processor that will be able to help them to write flawlessly.

8. Sound Literacy

For younger children suffering from dyslexia, working with phonics is extremely important. Sound Literacy is a very fun app that has game-like activities that are created in order to help students learn to recognize letter sounds.

9. Dyslexia Quest

This is an app that feels and looks a lot like a game, but is created to help the dyslexic child work on their memory skills, sequencing, and phonics, which are all skills that dyslexics struggle with.

10. Natural Reader

Reading texts, web pages, and emails can be difficult for dyslexic children as well. However, there are a lot of text-to-speech apps that end up sounding very mechanical and feel clunky. Natural Readers provides them with a nice, natural-sounding voice that can help them to read many different documents.

11. Learning Ally

Learning Ally is an amazing resource for audiobooks. This app is filled with hundreds of books for children available through a monthly subscription. Users are able to follow along and to adjust the size or type of text in order to make it easier for them to read.

#10

Celebrate

One of the most important things you should do when it comes to helping your child with dyslexia is to celebrate every little success. Dyslexic children struggle to do work simply because they feel it is too hard for them, even though they tend to be very smart, bright children. Celebration is one way to make sure they know that you are proud of them and that they are doing well. This will give them more confidence and will motivate them to continue putting in the hard work.

Celebrating success is a great way to encourage and nourish a child's growth and progress. By praising all of their success, no matter how big or small, you can unlock a powerful tool to connect with and support your child to continue their development.

As a parent, it doesn't get more exciting than when you get to see your child overcome obstacles and start taking risks, whether they know they are doing it or not. Bother the milestones and their accomplishments show you how far they have come. While it may be discouraging for them to hit bumps in the road during their life, parents are the child's number one advocate. Because of this, parents feel that they are responsible when their child does experience delays.

Other Types of Success

What often comes to mind when talking about what builds a child's self-esteem are the bigger achievements in their life, like making the baseball team, winning a contest, or getting a part in the school play. However, when fifth graders, all of whom had learning disabilities of some kind, were asked about things they have done that they feel good about, and some interesting facts came to light. They didn't simply list off the big achievements, but they started getting good grades, doing well in math, or getting a good test score. It isn't a big surprise as to why these accomplishments help their self-esteem.

These children also let them in on some smaller, and less noticeable successes. There are successes that other kids naturally assume will occur or ones adults don't think about acknowledging, such as:

- ☆ Knowing friends will still like you even when you have to go to a special education class

- ☆ Making a new friend

☆ Actually finishing a school project

☆ Getting homework finished on time

☆ Making it to the next grade because I didn't think I could

☆ Finishing the school year and being able to relax during the summer

Children who have learning disabilities tend not to take social or academic achievements for granted. These types of accomplishments tend not to come as easily for them as they do for others, and, because of this, makes them a good cause for celebration. After all, it is these "quieter" successes that add up, especially when it comes to their self-esteem.

There are also actions that parents and teachers alike take for granted, but can improve your child's self-esteem. For most, these actions are instinctive. However, it is best if you remind yourself every not and then, as they can easily be ignored or forgotten in day-to-day life.

☆ Teach all children that everybody's brain is different and that we all learn in different ways

☆ Recognize the child's good ideas

☆ Give lots of compliments and "put ups" and not "put downs"

☆ Don't yell

☆ Take time to explain things, especially new ideas

Benefits of Celebration

Genuine and enthusiastic celebration has the biggest impact on your child's success. Regardless of the way you choose to celebrate, and you should think about ways that are age and developmentally appropriate, there is bound to be a significant amount of change in your child's life as well as yours.

For your child, praise shows progress. When you take the time to cherish all of their achievements, you teach them about the things that you are proud of and what you want to do more of. It is going to be a special time that the two of you share, and you will establish a safe place for them to continue growing.

For you, it is simply fun to celebrate. The more you do this, the more motivation and energy you are going to have to navigate through yours and your child's journey. Plus, working on your ability to present for your child will develop lifelong benefits for the two of you.

How to Celebrate

Everybody is different. Your child may not like big, loud, or energetic displays of excitement, even if you feel that they deserve that kind of praise. If that be the case, think about other ways to celebrate that works well for them. You can do this in many different ways. Knowing the best way to celebrate a child's success, without going overboard, can be a challenge.

1. Take Time

Trying to find time to celebrate can seem impossible or sometimes forgotten within all of the chaos for the week. This is why it is so important to acknowledge their accomplishments as soon as you can. Providing your child with your full and undivided attention is often what they want. That, and a hug, can go a long way when it comes to celebrating their successes.

2. Tell Others

With our age of social media, it is very common to share your child's achievements with friends on Instagram and Facebook. But are there some people that your child would like to share their successes with? What might be better than using social media is to text a picture or FaceTime with family and friends to share the good news. Encouraging words from the grandparents about their good grades is great for them to hear, and FaceTimeing them about how well the week went at school helps to acknowledge this accomplishment and lets the grandparents know about all of their positives.

3. Display It

Depending on how old they are, displaying their awards or work is one way for them to feel that what they have done is worthy of being viewed. You can buy a set of inexpensive frames that you can use as a rotating display of awards and pictures. You can also hang up a corkboard where older children can hang up things like medals or ribbons. Also, you can't forget about the refrigerator. That is always a great place to hang artwork, report cards, and photos. You can also put up a chalkboard in a high-traffic area in your home. This can be used as a headline board to announce their accomplishment.

4. Special Meal

Getting to pick out a special treat or meal can be a very special treat to celebrate success. This could be choosing something for dessert, picking out a restaurant for dinner, or having a favorite meal for dinner at home, followed by a game night or family movie are all great options. Your child is going to enjoy this opportunity to pick their celebration.

5. Form Traditions

Repeating certain things often get boring, but when something fun is repeated, it gets called a tradition. Maybe there is a plate that is gets used only during special occasions, or a tablecloth that is used at certain times. Celebrating accomplishments should be a tradition, and including some sort of physical element or activity, such as a dance night, can make things memorable.

6. Physical Rewards

While there is a lot of controversy over giving money or a gift to a child as a reward, there are times when it can be a great way to celebrate hard work. Good grades could equal money in the bank for college. A gift could be something that will help in the program that they are a part of works. If the reward you give them can help them to continue achieving, it will also help to celebrate their accomplishment.

From displaying work to supportive words, it is very simple and easy to take a few moments to make your child feel special about what they have achieved. There tends to be very little cost to acknowledge these important moments. When parents and others acknowledge hard work, it is encouraging and meaningful for children.

How Not To Celebrate

While celebration is very important for your child, there is a wrong way to do it. This isn't something that most parents will think about, but these mistakes can place unnecessary pressure on the child or cause them to feel afraid to fail in the future. Instead, you need to make sure that the celebrations and praise provide your child with encouragement and confidence to accomplish more. Here are some things to keep in mind to make sure that you don't end up creating stress for your child.

1. Don't Belittle Others

If your child has been successful in something recently, then there is a good chance that there are other kids who weren't as successful. While it is important to praise your child, it is just as important not to put those less successful children down. A good example of this is when parents make fun of the losing team at a sporting event. But it can also including putting down students who made a lower grade on a test. You never want to teach your child to be nasty or arrogant when they are successful. You want them to be gracious and humble. You should always avoid making a comparison, and simply focus on your child individually. This is especially true if you have multiple children. Treat each child as their own person.

2. Celebrate Their Results AND Their Effort

Your child is not going to be perfect at everything they do, but as long as they are doing their best, you should provide them with support and congratulation. This is the best way to teach your child the importance of perseverance and hard work. There will come a day when your child will face something that proves to be a bit too hard for them to win against, but it will be important that you celebrate the effort that they put into trying to overcome the obstacle. You should not place all of the emphasis on results, and remember to stress how important it is to do things to the best of your ability.

3. Have a Personal and Broad Definition of Success

As a parent, it is very important that you don't define success in a narrow manner, such as the final grade in a class. Not only is this going to place too much pressure on your child, who already faces more stress in school than the average child, but it will also prevent you from seeing other accomplishments they make as they learn and grow. Maybe they didn't get the A+ you had hoped for at the end of the semester, but their grades still improved dramatically throughout the semester. Even if they still struggle, they may have had a couple of big wins, or maybe they did their best at staying the course and not giving up when things got hard. There are many different ways to define success, and to make sure that you are noticing how they are finding their own success.

4. Don't Make your Love and Affection Dependant of Success

One of the worst ways a parent can celebrate success for any child, and not just those with dyslexia, is to only show them love and affection during times of big success. You may not have to praise them for every little thing they do, but you should make sure that your support and love are unconditional. You want your child to know that you are always in their corner no matter if they win or lose, and that you can more about them than the outcome of things. Only praising them when they succeed or win is just cruel, and it places way too much pressure on them. You have to be proud of them first, and their accomplishments second. You want to improve your relationship with them, not cause them to resent you for the rest of their lives.

Famous People With Dyslexia

The main thing that celebration looks to do is to motivate your child to continue trying their best. While this may not be a celebration, another great way to motivate your child is to let them know that they aren't the only ones. This information is something that you may want to use when they are struggling and can't seem to find the will to keep trying. Share with them that even celebrities face the struggles of dyslexia. Here are a few examples you can use:

☆ Whoopi Goldberg

Many years before Whoopi Goldberg ever got her dyslexia diagnosis, and before she learned how commonly in occurred, kids she went to school with would call her "dumb." Her mother would always tell her that she shouldn't listen to them. Her mom encouraged her to be whatever she wanted to be. Goldberg believed what her mother said, and grew up to be an actress, talk show host, and comedian. And one of only around a dozen people who has won an Emmy, Grammy, Academy Award, and a Tony. She says that thinking differently is what has helped her succeed.

☆ Steven Spielberg

The legendary film director Steven Spielberg didn't get his diagnosis of dyslexia until he was in his 60s. His school administrators often labeled him as lazy. His classmates also bullied him, and the troubles he had in school end up helping him in his career. Movies gave him a place to channel his energy, and feeling as if he were an outsider helped him to co-write *The Goonies*. He has stated that finding out that he has dyslexia was like "the last puzzle piece to a great mystery that I've kept to myself."

☆ Cher

The Grammy-winning singer and Academy Award-winning actress Cher struggled with an undiagnosed learning difference. In her autobiography *The First Time*, she wrote, "I couldn't read quickly enough to get all my homework done and for me, math was like trying to understand Sanskrit." She could only learn by listening to the teacher because couldn't comprehend what she read. She didn't find out that she had dyslexia until she took her child to get evaluated.

☆ Octavia Spencer

Octavia has won a Golden Globe and an Academy Award for her acting. She ended up writing children's books because she understands how challenging reading can be. This is because she has dyslexia. She remembers how scared she has been in school whenever she was asked to read out loud. "I was paralyzed with fear because I kept inverting words and dropping words," she said. However, she stresses the importance of not letting dyslexia prevent children from going after their dreams. "It doesn't really mean that you're not intelligent, it just means that your brain functions differently," she said.

☆ Tim Tebow

The former NFL quarterback, Tim Tebow, suffers from dyslexia. His father and brother suffer from it as well. Learning differences tend to run in families. He ended up getting the diagnosis while in elementary school and learned about many different ways to work around their reading difficulties. He has said, "It has to do with finding out how you learn."

☆ Keira Knightley

After getting diagnosed with dyslexia at age six, Keira Knightley used her love for action to motivate her to read. She made a deal with her parents that if she focused on her reading some every single day, that they would hire her an agent. She made good on her half, using scripts to help practice her reading.

☆ Jennifer Aniston

Jennifer Aniston may be known for her role as Rachel in *Friends*, but she has also been living with dyslexia. She didn't find out about her diagnosis until she was in her 20s. She said that finding out explained why it had been so hard for her to read back in school, and the reason why she decided to be the class clown instead of a teacher's pet. Her diagnosis answered a bunch of questions.

The next time your kid is feeling down, help lift their spirits by pulling this information out. Reassure them that despite having reading and learning difficulties, these celebrities overcame their struggles to become successful.

Another way to use celebrities to help your child out is to have them make a vision board. Research dyslexic celebrities with your child and have them pick out one that they look up to. They can then create a vision board with the celebrity on it along with information about how the celebrity worked through their dyslexia. Whenever they start feeling down, have them go to their board to remind them that anything is possible. They aren't dumb, stupid, lazy, or any other negative word others might use. They are just as smart and bright as the rest of their peers; they simply think in a different way.

Conclusion

Thank you for making it through to the end of the book, let's hope it was informative and able to provide you with all of the tools you need to achieve your goals whatever they may be.

The next step is to start using these techniques with your child. Show them the support they need and work with them. One on one attention is important for a dyslexic child, and while it can get frustrating, refrain from getting upset with them. Your child is doing the best they can, and you can trust that they are likely just as frustrated, if not more so. If you haven't already, get a routine established for them and set aside some time each day to help them with their homework. Just remember, with the right tools, all goals are achievable.

Finally, if you found this book useful in any way, a review on Amazon is always appreciated!

Other books by Angie Turner

ADHD - tools for kids

ADHD is not the result of ineffective parenting education, and it is not related to the "badness" of the child.

ADHD is an attention disorder that if not managed right can become a real problem, for the individual himself, for the family and school, with discomforts and frustration at school and personal level.

Angie Turner is a tutor for children with learning disabilities and in " ADHD - tools for kids" she wants to explain to you how is possible to obtain important results.

https://www.amazon.com/dp/B088TVGMNH